The
POWER
of
MENTORSHIP

THE
MASTERMIND
GROUP

www.The PowerOfMentorship.com
www.DonBoyer.org
www.DonBoyerAuthor.com

THE POWER OF MENTORSHIP
THE MASTERMIND GROUP
Published by Real Life Teaching/Publishing

DonBoyer@ReaLifeTeaching.com
www.DonBoyer.org
www.DonBoyerAuthor.com
562-789-1909
Whittier, California

Copyright © 2009 Real Life Teaching/Publishing
Library of Congress Control Number 2009903550
ISBN 978-1-61539-401-2

Cover Design by www.KillerGraffix.com

Editing, Composition, and Typography by www.ProEditingService.com

This book is available at quantity discounts for bulk purchase.

For more information contact: Real Life Teaching/Publishing
DonBoyer@ReaLifeTeaching.com
Telephone: 562-789-1909
Whittier, California

Special Note: This edition of *The Power of Mentorship The Mastermind Group* is designed to provide information and motivation to our readers. It is sold with the understanding that the publisher is not engaged to render any type of psychological, legal, or any other kind of professional advice. The content of each article is the sole expression and opinion of its author, and not necessarily that of the publisher. No warranties or guarantees are expressed or implied by the publisher's choice to include any of the content in this volume. Neither the publisher nor the individual author(s) shall be liable for any physical, psychological, emotional, financial, or commercial damages, including but not limited to special, incidental, consequential or other damages. Our views and rights are the same: You are responsible for your own choices, actions, and results.

Printed in the United States of America

Dedication

This book is dedicated to all those who are willing to think big, dream big and live large. For those rare individuals who dare to step out of the limiting beliefs of the masses and choose to adhere themselves to the group of achievers who are dedicated to making a positive impact on this generation and those to come.

Inside of you is greatness; dare to let it out!

ACKNOWLEDGMENT

When you look at great accomplishments what you are really seeing is the combination of effort, gifts, talents and skills of a magnificent team. There is no such thing as a Lone Ranger super star. You will find that there is no "I" in the word success because success is always a by-product of a team. Everything that has been done in the Power of Mentorship community is the result of all our fantastic mentors.

Words can not express my gratitude for the following people who made this book a living reality:

Our Lord, Jesus Christ
My wife and life partner, Melinda Boyer
My Mentor, Bob Proctor
Mick and Manisha Moore
Our editor, Paulette Bethel
George and Olivia Ramirez

All the co-authors and Mentors who contributed their knowledge to this book:

Bob Proctor	Colleen Clarke
Marie Diamond	George Ramirez
Brian Tracy	Zig Ziglar
Elizabeth George	Mick Moore
Jim Noll	Lianna Marie
Susan Stewart	Don Staley
Doug Vermeeren	Kim Adams

All of you are my true Pillars of Success!

TABLE OF CONTENTS

The Power of Mentorship The Mastermind Group

INTRODUCTION

Napoleon Hill once said, "Analyze the record of any man who has accumulated a great fortune, and many of those who have accumulated modest fortunes, and you will find that they have either consciously, or unconsciously employed the 'Master Mind' principle."

What is a mastermind group?

Napoleon Hill, author of *Think and Grow Rich*, first defined the mastermind as a "coordination of knowledge and effort, in a spirit of harmony, between two or more people, for the attainment of a definite purpose."

Hill's concept of the "Master Mind" was inspired by Andrew Carnegie, wealthy steel magnate. According to Hill: "Mr. Carnegie's Master Mind group consisted of a staff of approximately fifty men, with whom he surrounded himself, for the DEFINITE PURPOSE of manufacturing and marketing steel. He attributed his entire fortune to the POWER he accumulated through this 'Master Mind.'"

Since the publication of *Think and Grow Rich* in 1937, the idea of mastermind groups has grown and evolved to become a staple tool of successful individuals.

The benefits of having a mastermind group are far reaching:

1. You have a set of people available to help you succeed.

2. You get the benefit of differing perspectives, ideas and concepts.

3. Your mastermind team can bring resources and connections to the table you might not have had on your own.

4. You receive information, motivation and inspiration from those in your group.

As I have always said; "Who you listen to determines where you go and what you end up with in life."

Napoleon Hill even went so far as to say there was a mystical quality created when a mastermind group was formed. He said: "No two minds ever come together without, thereby, creating a third, invisible, intangible force which may be likened to a third mind."

In other words, your ability to create things in the world is increased by having that invisible "third mind" of the mastermind group.

Now, in this powerful edition of the *Power of Mentorship and the Master Mind Group,* you, the reader have the benefit of having some of the top leaders in the 21st century sharing with you the concepts, ideas and experiences that help them achieve extraordinary success, create lasting relationships, develop powerful connections, enjoy dynamic health and teach you that when you hit a set back, you do not sit back; you jump up and make a come back!

I encourage you to read, and then read again, every chapter

until the knowledge of these mentors sinks deeply into your mind and they become yours.

Reach out and contact these mentors and they will reach out to you!

Don and Melinda Boyer
Publisher

Bob Proctor has, for 40 years, focused his entire agenda around helping people create lush lives of prosperity, rewarding relationships and spiritual awareness.

Bob Proctor knows how to help you because he comes from a life of want and limitation himself. In 1960, he was a high-school dropout with a resume of dead-end jobs and a future clouded in debt. One book was placed in his hands—Napoleon Hill's *Think and Grow Rich*—which planted the seed of hope in Bob's mind. In just months, and with further support from the works of Earl Nightingale, Bob's life literally spun on a dime. In a year, he was making more than $100,000 and soon topped the $1 million mark.

It doesn't matter how you grew up, or what you've struggled with in life—your mind is unscathed by any circumstance you've struggled with in life—your mind is unscathed by any circumstance you've yet lived... and it's phenomenally powerful! Let Bob Proctor's live seminars, best-selling books and recordings show you how to excavate the wonderful gem of your own mind.

Visit Bob Proctor online at www.BobProctor.com

CHAPTER ONE
It's Easy to Earn Money
By Bob Proctor

It is a real possibility that everything you and I have been taught about how to earn money is so far from the truth that it's almost comical. Earning money has nothing to do with age, formal education, gender or geography. It has nothing to do with past experience or your formal years of education or your level of intellect. There are individuals who are functionally illiterate who have become multimillionaires, while there are others who are absolutely brilliant and they are broke. Virtually anyone can be taught how to earn millions of dollars and yet the sad truth is that 97 out of every 100 people are born, live their entire lives, and die without ever learning how to earn money. To perpetuate this ridiculous problem, their ignorance is passed along from one generation to the next.

Our school system has been designed as an environment to enlighten young minds, to replace ignorance with understanding and ultimately improve the quality of life. And though our educational system has obviously been successful in many areas, it has woefully neglected one important subject, "How to Earn Money." A lack of understanding in this area is the cause of numerous unwanted and unnecessary problems, since money is the medium of exchange that is used worldwide for other people's products and services.

There has always been a small, select group, approximately

3% of our population, who clearly understand that prosperity consciousness is the primary cause of wealth and their prosperity consciousness, like ignorance, is also passed down from one generation to the next.

Let's look at "money." What is it? Money is a reward you receive for the service you render. The more valuable the service, the greater the reward. Thinking of ways we can be of greater service will not only help us earn more money, it will also enable us to grow intellectually and spiritually.

MONEY IS AN IDEA

The paper you fold and place in your purse or pocket is not money. It is paper with ink on it. It represents money, but it is not money. Money is an idea. The earning of money has nothing to do with the paper stuff, it has to do with consciousness.

To accumulate wealth, a person must become very comfortable with the idea of money. That may sound strange, however, most people are not comfortable with the idea of money, which is why they do not have any. The cause of poverty is poverty consciousness. A poverty consciousness will cause a person to see, hear, think and feel ... lack and limitation.

The late Mike Todd said, "Being broke is a temporary situation. Being poor is a mental state."

He was correct. There are wealthy people who lose every

cent they have through a series of mistakes in judgment, but that does not make them poor. They will have it all back in a short time because of their prosperity consciousness.

Many years ago, George Bernard Shaw expressed his thoughts on money. People have such strong views on both of these statements, I purposely use them in my seminars to cause the attendees to think.

1. It is the duty of every person to be rich.
2. It is a sin to be poor.

Before you reject these as being ridiculous, let's analyze them. To fully understand what Shaw was saying, you must have an open mind. There is a law that states everything is moving, absolutely nothing rests. You are either moving ahead in life or going in reverse... growing or dying... creating or disintegrating, becoming richer or poorer.

There is another law to which people often refer in many different ways... Karmic Law... Sowing and Reaping... Cause and Effect... Action, Re-Action. How you refer to this law is of little importance relative to your understanding of how it works.

The thoughts, feelings, and actions that you express in life are seeds that you sow. The conditions, circumstances and things that come into your life are the harvest you reap as a RESULT of the seeds that you sow. For a moment, store this information in the back of your mind while we investigate the deeper understanding of the words SIN and MONEY.

Sin is... transgression of the law. Violating the law is a sin and, in truth, the price of sin is death. That does not mean your heart will stop beating, but it does mean you will regress. I previously mentioned there is a law that states you will either create or disintegrate, you will grow or die. When you attempt to "get" without giving, you are trying to reap the harvest without sowing the seeds, and it will not work.

Now let's look at "money." What is it? Money is a reward you receive for the service you render; the more valuable the service, the greater the reward. Attempting to "get" money without providing service is also a violation of the law.

Shaw believed you and I are here to serve one another. Thinking of ways we can be of greater service will enable us to grow intellectually and spiritually. It is our duty to serve and money is a reward we receive for that service. If a person has received their money in an unlawful manner—by law, they must pay the price; you reap what you sow.

In light of the laws that govern our universe, what Shaw said is correct. However, if a person is not consciously thinking, Shaw's statements would appear very callous, even ridiculous. Personally, I believe Shaw made those statements the way he did, to provoke people to think.

Quite simply, what Shaw was emphasizing was the importance of our own responsibility in the quest for abundance. Abundance is something we magnetize

14

ourselves to... we draw it into our lives... in every aspect of our lives. Business associates, friends, everything we want will come into our life by law, not luck. You are either attracting or repelling good. It is your own consciousness that ultimately determines your results.

"Money is in consciousness and it must be earned." If you want to improve your financial position in life, focus your attention on creating a higher level of prosperity consciousness. Begin by preparing a powerful, positive affirmation and fuel it with emotion. When you do this, you are depositing this creative energy in the treasury of your subconscious mind. And, by repeating this process over and over and over again every day, it will begin to alter your conditioning and mentally move you in the direction you want to go. Write it out, read it, feel it, and let it take hold of your mind.

How much money do you want? Saying you want more is not good enough. Five dollars is more. How much more? Decide on a figure. Be specific. You will not seriously want more money than you are capable of earning... however, you would be wise to remember, you must earn it.

THERE ARE THREE INCOME EARNING STRATEGIES

Trading time for money—By far the worst of the three income earning strategies, it is employed by approximately 96% of our population—doctors, lawyers, accountants, laborers, etc. There is an inherent problem with this strategy—saturation. You run out of time. If a person accumulates any degree of wealth employing this strategy,

15

it will be at the expense of a life. They compromise on the car they drive, the house they live in, the clothes they choose and the vacations they take. They rarely, if ever, get what they want.

Investing money to earn money—This strategy is used by approximately 3% of the population. The number is small for the obvious reason—very few people have any money to invest. Many people who effectively employ this strategy follow the advice of a trusted, knowledgeable advisor.

Leveraging yourself to earn money—This is where you multiply your time through the efforts of others by setting up Multiple Sources of Income (MSIs). This is, without question, the very best way to increase your income. Make a decision to have many sources of income; it's the strategy that wealthy people have used dating clear back to the ancient Babylonians. Unfortunately, this strategy is only used by approximately 1% of our population, yet that 1% earns approximately 96% of all the money that is earned! You are only a decision away from membership.

Once you determine how much money you want to earn, write it down on a sheet of paper in large figures. Look at the number with the dollar sign beside it and tell yourself over and over again: THAT AMOUNT OF MONEY IS AN EFFECT. IT REPRESENTS A REWARD THAT I WANT TO RECEIVE. WHAT SERVICE CAN I RENDER THAT WOULD BE DESERVING OF THAT REWARD?

Take the total figure and divide it into multiple parts.

Let each part represent a source of income. Each source of income represents a separate reward that you would receive for a service you would render. Work on one source of income at a time; each one can become an exciting part of your life.

◎ Think of how you can do whatever you do— more effectively.

◎ Think of how you can improve the quality and quantity of service you render.

◎ Think of how you can help people in a greater way.

Money is a servant; the more you earn, the more you can help others.

Colleen Clarke is a highly regarded Corporate Trainer, Keynote Speaker and Career Specialist in the areas of networking, communication and career management/transition including assessment tools and workplace issues. She is the author of *Networking How to Build Relationships That Count* and *How to Find a Job and Keep It.*

Colleen is the Workplace Forum Advisor for Monster.ca and a guest columnist for Canada's national newspaper, *The Globe and Mail*. Always motivating and humorous, Colleen has inspired and edu-trained thousands of individuals and groups to career excellence. Check out her web site at www.colleenclarke.com.

CHAPTER TWO
If You're Not Appearing, You Are Disappearing
By Colleen Clarke

I'm going out to make some new friends, so they are there when I need them later on.

It's funny, you know. Everyday you get up and get ready for work, arrive, do your job and go home. The whole time you are at work, you are making an impression of one kind or another through your visibility factor. Whether you are in the lunch room, walking down the hall or sitting at your desk, people in your work environment are noticing you, probably more so than you are noticing yourself.

I bet no one has ever asked himself at the end of the day, "How visible was I to my colleagues and superiors today?"

So, let's think about it. What impact **would** higher visibility have on your job? How much more effective and efficient would you be if more people knew who you were and what you did? How much more productive and happy would you be if you knew more people and what they did?

Whether you represent a company or are a company, your visibility factor is a marketing tool you need to take out of your tool box and sharpen almost daily. In 1990, at the start of a six year recession, I started a networking support group for unemployed business professionals called

19

E.A.R.N., the Executive Advancement Resource Network. Men and women from every walk of life met to provide weekly support, contacts and job leads to each other, with the premise that networking accounts for 75-80% of all job leads.

As the founder and administrator/facilitator I was frequently being interviewed by all media forms extolling the wonderment of this amazing group of professionals and the organization. When I founded E.A.R.N., I made a major career change from marketing and sales to career counseling and workshop delivery. My media visibility not only helped bring in members but also provided E.A.R.N. with office equipment and supply donations. Professionally, my new career took off; every week I had a captive audience of potential clients sitting right in front of me and running E.A.R.N. gave me credibility and validity in the career transition world.

10 years, 7000 clients and E.A.R.N. attendees later, with a fairly established career counseling and training profession on the go, the economy changed, attendance at E.A.R.N. dwindled and I decided to leave the organization I had founded. As you can imagine, I immediately lost my high profile. My visibility waned considerably except for a web site. I was greatly concerned about disappearing from the marketplace entirely. Believe me, in the largest city in Canada, that isn't hard to do.

I realized immediately that I had to do something to keep myself visible. A free commuter newspaper had first hit the streets of Toronto just as I was leaving E.A.R.N.

I called the editor-in-chief for months, leaving messages, asking if they would publish a career related article I had written that I thought would be perfect for the paper. Three months after I started leaving messages I got a call asking me to submit the column for the next day's paper. A week later the editor said they wanted to add a career column to the paper and would I be their weekly career columnist.

For the next eight years I wrote a weekly column that was read by half a million plus readers a day. A year after I started with the paper I approached Monster.ca, an Internet job site, about writing for them. Within two days I had my own page on Monster.ca and, to this day, I answer letters from people all over the world in my advice column and forum site, "Ask Colleen." Whew, it could have been a crashing end to a short but brilliant career. Instead, with a bit of ingenuity and a lot of determination I now had, not only local but, international recognition.

The concept of networking outside your immediate business circle dates back to the "old boys clubs" in merry old England, several centuries ago. The idea of networking internally is still coming into its own. The larger the organization, the easier it is to get lost in the hallowed halls of office politics and numbered employees.

The idea of everyone in an office randomly walking around their building, on all the floors, approaching total strangers and introducing themselves seems a tad odd, but not if you do so with purpose and intent.

The most important emotional intelligent skill required in the workplace today is one's ability to build and maintain interpersonal relationships. And, what better place to start, than in your own company?

Self employed entrepreneurs are the most proficient at networking and they realize that networking isn't just who you know, it's who knows you! Visibility and marketing are best achieved through a myriad of activities and contact networks from associations to business web sites. It is a daily activity for the self employed individual to gain and maintain much needed exposure; so why not employed people as well?

With an entrepreneurial attitude inside a company you heighten your credibility and visibility as an 'Intrapreneur'… a necessary rank for ambitious and forward thinking professionals. Intrapreneurs work with the gusto, passion and drive of an entrepreneur but within the confines of an organization. They perform their job like it is their company they are working in and their money that is on the line. Check out author Gifford Pinchot's book, *"Intrapreneuring: Why you Don't Have to Leave Your Corporation to Become an Entrepreneur,"* for more insights on working like an intrapreneur.

During economic slowdowns, people have a tendency to keep their heads down and their noses to the grind stone. If you extend your tentacles to every corner of the organization you can build allies, uncover inside information and identify opportunities before anyone else. When you choose internal networking as your plan of action you can also promote your department's viability and the contributions being made to the company as part of the whole.

Increasing your area of influence allows opportunities to find you. The more people who know about your *'Professional Wonderment,'* obvious and hidden, the better. High visibility allows you to collaborate with other departments to strengthen your causes and accomplish more with greater support. Rifling through your data base management system or business cards to locate the perfect in-house person to help out in an emergency, or in a pinch, is immediate, compared to using the yellow pages or the Internet, and much more reliable.

Over my life time I had the good fortune to be hired into companies where my skill set filled the white spaces in the org chart. With your finger on the pulse of all company goings on, you can be the one to identify opportunities that are often overlooked, in good times or bad.

This is where I must remind you to ensure that the grapevine, at a minimum, knows your skill set and what you bring to the table. It is not enough for your 'guardian angel' to know your skills and strengths; the arterial network within the company must know them as well.

Heightening Visibility Through an Internal Network

Okay, it's time to start executing your visibility plan, to do some internal networking that will strengthen your relationships and build trust among your colleagues, subordinates and superiors.

1. Identify a group within the organization that allows you to showcase your talents. The group can be Toastmasters, a women's networking group, Weight Watchers, a social committee, the United Way or any likeminded group with an interest in finances, music, books, arts, sports, culture, etc. Join a group that allows you to use your hidden talents. You may work in the accounting department, but if you have a propensity for fund raising or marketing, get on that committee.

Never mind eating lunch at your desk. You don't meet people or do your brain or body any good hiding in your cubicle or behind a closed door. While wandering the halls of your organization, take the initiative and ask a new somebody to lunch or drinks after work, or to join your interest group.

2. Ask people you know to introduce you to people you don't know, and reciprocate introductions to others as well. More than likely you don't know who you don't know or whom you should know. Keep in mind that networking is about give and take so you want to keep your eyes and ears open for people you can help as well as people who can help meet your objectives. You just never know who people are related to or who they know—ask!

3. If you want to make a friend or ally for life,

complement them about a recent accomplishment in front of colleagues. You needn't make a big deal about it but bringing attention to others is a great way for people to remember your gracious spirit, and in turn, they may want to do things for you.

4. When in groups or conversing one on one, listen. Listen for what others want or need to make their lives easier, be it a resource, information or a person. Tell them you will keep your ears open and you will let them know as soon as you've uncovered the solution. Knowing you are on their side makes people feel supported and validated.

5. Don't just join a group, sit on a committee. Get to know people throughout the company on a more intimate level than just their name, title and department. I was on a not for profit board where all the women on the board were also in a book club so they were tied to each other through more than one commonality. When you get to know people outside their realm of expertise and their position you see them for more than their job description, and visa versa.

6. Find out the hobbies and out of office passions of your colleagues. Some people are involved in the most interesting personal activities that could lead you to a new adventure and a whole new group of people, ergo, contacts and resources.

7. Listen to audio book tapes and attend seminars, in house and externally, and share your learnings with your boss and colleagues.

8. Offer to conduct in-house training sessions on a skill at which you excel. Offer to hold a workshop on a hobby or area of interest where you would teach others the likes of painting, guitar playing or yoga.

9. Offer to be a guest speaker at a conference or seminar of your industry association. If speaking isn't your bailiwick, offer to write an article for an internal or association newsletter. Offer to cover seminars at a conference, interview each presenter and write a synopsis of their presentation to be sent out to all conference attendees. Be sure to ask the publisher to include your photo where possible, but definitely a short by-line with your name, title and employer.

10. Volunteer to work industry trade shows. Standing behind a booth at a trade show and circulating to other booths is pure high visibility. Be sure to look like a million dollars, be right up to date on the product or service being marketed and make a point of speaking to as many guests as you can.

11. Attend whatever in house seminars you can. Aside from the professional development aspect of these workshops, meeting new people from various departments is fun and interesting; to say the least... and you never know who knows whom.

When you enter a room, arrive early enough to introduce yourself to the speaker, and then sit close to someone in the audience that looks interesting to you. Sit either one or two seats to the right or left of them, or a row behind or in front. Take the initiative by chatting about the topic of the session or asking open ended questions about that person's interest in attending the session. As the room fills up you can move closer to your new friend. Try to find a common ground as chit chat has a tendency to dwindle quite quickly. Exchange business cards or emails and promise to connect again after the session. The follow up is as important as the initial connection.

12. Make casual conversation with people in common areas like lunch rooms, kitchens, board rooms and cloak rooms about market occurrences, industry related news, and strategic planning. Bring your lunch and eat in different areas of the office or building. When you eat alone it is easier to chat people up who are in your proximity. Don't restrict yourself to the company lunchroom. When possible, eat in local parkettes, outdoor quads between buildings, near planters or even on the stairs in front of your building.

13. Be the ice breaker when standing in line every morning at your local java shop. Chances are the same people are lining up at the same time and place every day.

14. You want to be collecting business cards from all the people you are meeting. The etiquette of business card exchange is that you ask for someone's card after you have had a short visit. You do not offer your card, you ask for theirs. Follow up with each meeting and then twice a year go through the cards

and make contact again if you feel it worthwhile. Email makes staying in touch so much easier and is often more expedient than phoning, though consider calling people whom you want to really be connected with.

15. Volunteer to introduce a senior executive at an AGM or company retreat. There may not be many opportunities in which you can meet, let alone get noticed, by the "ivory tower execs" so look for opportunities for them to put a face to a name.

16. Leave post-it notes on computer screens or chairs to acknowledge colleagues' accomplishments or a rough time they are going through.

17. Comprise a list of key people within the organization that you would like to meet. Ask everyone you know if they might know any of the people on your list.

18. Connecting one person to another is so rewarding and always greatly appreciated. Find out the business goals and objectives of your colleagues and try to line them up with people who can help solve their problems.

19. When providing customer service or collaborating with suppliers or customers, ask for their perceptions of your company and the industry. You can chat casually or actually introduce the subject: "I'd like to ask your opinion about something, if I may."

Visibility can be as simple as building a personal/business

relationship with your contacts so they see you in action
and really know, first hand, what your offerings are.

By the way, thank you for reading this and helping me
build my visibility.

 **Marie Diamond** is an internationally known Feng Shui Master and one of the top transformational leaders in the world, consulting with and teaching people in more than 30 countries.

Marie has connected with numerous Hollywood celebrities, major film directors, and producers, music giants, and famous authors. She has been featured in several TV and film projects including: The Secret, I Married a Princess, and The Jerry Hall Heaven and Earth Show.

Her current projects include writing books, creating several large real estate projects and the creation of an e-commerce site.

Contact Marie at 1-888-924-4488 or email Info@MarieDiamond.com or read her blog at: http://mariediamondblog.blogspot.com.

CHAPTER THREE
The Law of Attraction and Feng Shui
By Marie Diamond

In the hit movie, *The Secret*, I was featured as one of the teachers. Since then, many people ask me what Feng Shui has to do with The Law of Attraction.

Feng Shui is well known as an art of placement based on several Chinese philosophical principles, such as Yin Yang Balance, the cycles of the five elements, etc. But it is, indeed, more than just that.

My Personal History
When I started studying Feng Shui at 15 years old, I was already consciously aware of the Laws of the Universe. I started practicing them at seven years old by drawing on paper in beautiful colors the images that I wished to manifest. At 15 years, I had a year of bad luck, being in three major accidents. At school, I was daily teased and bullied. I had no friends and was almost killed by a truck.

I asked my spiritual master, "What am I doing wrong? I have been a straight A student, I have been doing my Christian practices daily and using my knowledge of the Law of Attraction. Still, I attract such bad luck. I was desperate.

Sound familiar? You do all the right things and still you get nowhere.

Bad Feng Shui

My Master told me, "You have bad Feng Shui. You sleep in the wrong direction, your bedroom is in the wrong area of your parents home, your personal bathroom is in your personal relationship direction, your huge closet blocks your personal health direction, and you have the wrong color and style of wallpaper."

He suggested that I move to my older brothers room, which was empty. I needed to paint the room in an orange color and paint the furniture white. He asked me to sleep towards the southwest and face my desk to the west. He also advised me to hang wonderful pictures of friends and romance in my personal relationship direction and place images of healthy looking women in my personal health direction.

Results

Knowing my Master, I did exactly what he told me and within one month received these results:

- I experienced love at first sight with the most handsome guy I've ever met.
- As I started to date him, I became very popular and everyone wanted to be my friend to be close to him.
- The bullying stopped.
- My health improved drastically and I didn't have accidents anymore.

I started experiencing that there is more to the Law of Attraction than what I knew. I experienced that as you are one with the universe, the universe is not only your body, mind, and soul, but it is also the home and environment you live in. The thoughts, feelings, and actions in your environment reflected by the images you choose to place around you, creates another level of attraction.

Grandmaster
Later on, when I started intensely studying Feng Shui, I heard a Grandmaster share that there are three levels of good luck and that Feng Shui is more than an art of placement: it is also the science of quantum physics of the environment.

There are three aspects of the Law of Attraction. The first level is called Heavenly Luck. When you are born in this life, the Law of Attraction is already at work. You attracted your parents, your country of birth, your time, your culture, your language, your talents, your race, etc. Some believe this is based on your previous life experiences and what you attracted in previous lives. Others will call it destiny and what God/the Universe chooses for you. But, as you are the universe, it was your choice, after all.

The Feng Shui Masters found out that this aspect is 33.3 percent at work in your life. Can you change this part? Well, let's be honest, you can change your attitude towards some of this and, perhaps, you can change some or all of this. How much of this 33.3 percent is great destiny is something you don't know. It unfolds as you are living your life.

You have to fully master the Laws of the Universe to change your destiny completely, but it is certainly possible.

Human Luck
The second level is called Human Luck. That is the part most self-improvement teachers and books talk about. It is about changing your human experience by changing your attitude, your thoughts, your beliefs, your feelings, and actions. What will you do with your heavenly luck? Will you use your talents for the greatest good and make the best of your destiny, or will you just live your life as the victim of your karma?

Human luck is also 33.3 percent of your Law of Attraction, and how much of this percentage is already in action in a positive way you really don't know. But daily use of the Laws of the Universe in a positive way in your thoughts, feelings and actions will definitely help you to have a high score on this.

Unknown Part of the Secret
The unknown part of *The Secret* in the western world is the last aspect called Earth Luck. This last 33.3 percent of good luck that you can tap into is the environment that you live and work in. You are not only the universe within you; you are also the universe around you. You and your home and workspace are part of the unified quantum field where you create and manifest your life.

The best part of this aspect is that you can affect this part of good luck much easier than the other two thirds. Changing your desk, your wallpaper, your colors, and your images can be done in a few seconds or hours. But changing your culture or changing your attitude is much more complex and challenging.

I remember my Feng Shui Grandmaster telling me, "Changing your earth luck will ultimately change your human luck, and at the end also your heavenly luck."

This message stayed with me till it dawned on me. Your environment co-creates your thoughts, feelings, and actions. So, your human luck will ultimately change; and if you start using them the right way, the Laws of the Universe can change your destiny.

What you have hanging around you will definitely shape your mind and feelings, and you will ultimately start acting from this perspective.

But there is more.

The universe is now and here; it has no time and space framework. You live and experience the gravity of space and the linearity of time. How can you bring these unlimited things and this limited experience in alignment?

Well, the Feng Shui Masters, quantum physics avant la lettre, understood something very unique. Based on your personal birthday, when your unlimited being came in to the time and space framework of this planet, every human being has four access portals in the 360 degree circle of life that can give you unlimited access to the universe.

These four energy portals are connected with success, health, relationships, and wisdom. The eight wind directions, each expressed in 45 degrees, create access to the unlimited field of creation. Knowing your birthday gives you the code which wind directions are the right ones for you to manifest. When you wish to know yours, send an email to Info@MarieDiamond.com or visit my website at www.MarieDiamond.com to find out your four best energy portals.

Placing your Requests

Once you know your four best directions and find their position in your office, your living room, and bedroom you can hang or place your requests to the universe in these areas. In the home study course Diamond Feng Shui, you can learn how to activate these four best directions appropriately.

Your environment is sending unconscious messages to the universe 24 hours a day, 7 days a week, even if you are not aware of it. Whatever has been in these four best directions has been influencing you constantly. When I walk in and check someone's home, I actually tell them what they have been attracting or, better, what their home has been attracting with them.

Let's say that you were born in a family of entrepreneurs; your destiny was to be a business person. You have studied and done all the right things, but your business is not taking off. I come in and see that your paper shredder and your garbage bin are in the 45 degrees angle of your office that is your success area.

What have you been saying to the universe? Whatever my destiny is, whatever I work for, please throw it in the garbage and shred all my contracts.

Doing the right things is not enough. Like the man in my story in the movie, *The Secret*, he did all the right things to have romance, but he had all these images out about women who were alone. Actually, these seven images were in the exact 45 degree angle of his personal relationship direction in seven different rooms of his home. So, wherever he turned, he sent the message to the universe: women are not interested in me. And that was what he created because his home was influencing his beliefs, his thoughts, and his feelings. That is exactly what he ultimately manifested. By changing the images, he changed his inner self, and he manifested a different outer self.

Missing Part
Are you starting to understand why Feng Shui is not only part of the Law of Attraction, it is the missing part? It helps you understand why your prayers, your meditations, and your requests have not been working well or are not answered fast enough.

It is possible that the Universe was receiving a completely opposite message through your environment and, therefore, from you. You, perhaps, sent out a conscious thought and feeling for some minutes but unconsciously you were sending out a different message, and that is the one that keeps manifesting.

Fast Manifestation
When people ask me how to manifest the things they want faster, I tell them to make sure you align your inner self with your outer self, your home and office. What you

wish needs to be reflected in your environment. Just see it as a constant email that is every second sent out to the universe. How can you not manifest what you constantly ask?

Now you understand the importance of Feng Shui in the Law of Attraction. Find out your four best directions and start placing the right messages out in your universe around you.

Creating Mentorship Through Your Environment

I will share with you how you can tell the universe about creating the power of mentorship. There are three Aspects I wish to explain. The first part is that your ultimate mentor is God/ the Universe; this is connected with your Heavenly Luck. How can you connect with this ultimate mentor, and how can you let him/her/it know that you are open to the advice, the gifts, and the mentorship of this ultimate mentor?

That is where prayer, mediation, and visualization come in. This is not the focus of my article, but it is still 33.3 percent of your mentorship. Honor the ultimate mentor in your life in whatever way feels right for you. You can do this according to your traditions, your religion, or by your own creative impulses.

Feng Shui is a science of compassion. Everything is accepted as long as it is right for you and right for others.

The second part, based on your human luck, is that this ultimate mentor works through people and that you need to tell the ultimate mentor that you are open to listen to the people that are expressing mentorship to you. God/ the universe works through people, books, messages, TV and radio, speeches. I am still full of wonder in the ways the universe finds to support us. My list of experiences of the how is very long, and I am sure you have your own WAW list.

The third part, based on your earth luck, is that your environment needs to reflect that you are open to the ultimate mentor and to the support of mentors reflected in your life.

Here are some tips on how you can change your environment to open your home and office and, therefore, yourself to the power of mentorship.

Open your home to the ultimate mentor: God/the Universe. Imagine you are God or the Universe and you are walking into your home or office. Do you have easy access, or do you have to climb over the boxes and cramp your way into your entrance? Make your entrance as wide as possible so the ultimate mentor can bring you all the advice and gifts you need to grow your business and to be a better human being. Don't hang a mirror opposite the front door or you saying to the ultimate mentor: get out, I don't need you; I can do it alone. Tell the universe that it is welcome and this door is always open to the ultimate mentor by placing above the doorframe inside your home an image that represents God or the universe. You can use an angel image, a letter of God, a quote from the Bible, a spiritual image, or a harmonic cross.

General Places for Mentors in Your Home

Even if you don't know your personal four best directions, you can always place images representing the ultimate mentor (like statues of angels, letters of God, the Koran, images of spiritual masters, this book on the Power of Mentorship and any other of Don Boyer's books) in the Northwest area of your living room, office, or bedroom.

While you are placing it there, use the power of intentions and ask to be supported by the Ultimate Mentor and anything that represents this energy.

Personal Place for Mentors in Your Home

Find out your personal wisdom direction by sending an email to info@mariediamond.com and place in the 45 degrees angle of your bedroom the best mentor for romantic luck. This can be a book like *Men are from Mars and Women are from Venus* by John Gray or anything that brings you romantic mentorship. You are sending the message out that you are open to be mentored and, therefore, growth in your personal romance.

Place in your living room in your personal wisdom direction symbols for social mentorship, more about how to live your life. It could be something like quotes from great philosophers or the Bible. You are sending the message out to the universe that you are open to be mentored to be a better human being.

In your office, you can place in your personal wisdom direction the business cards of your business mentors, like your business coach, or magazines like Fortune or any

40

magazine about your professional sector. You are sending the message out that you are open to be mentored to be the best in your professional life.

Georges Ramirez' background as an educator, business owner and entrepreneur has allowed him to travel to 26 countries and 35 states.

He is grateful to have been featured in the entire Power of Mentorship series of books. He has also co-starred in three movies, *The Power of Mentorship*, *Pass it On* and *The Art of Business*.

George is available as a "skills trainer" and keynote speaker. His program for creating more effective communicators is called "Present with Purpose" and is held monthly throughout the country. It is designed for presenters/public speakers or those who want to be.

Sharing Inspiration and Prosperity with all he meets is what George enjoys.

He resides in SoCal with his lovely wife and life partner of over 32 years, Olivia.

Contact info: 1.866.945.4730
email george@realifeteaching.com
www.georgeramirezauthor.com

CHAPTER FOUR
The Components of Wealth Revealed
By George Ramirez

Nowadays, everybody has an opinion about the economy. Even if they never paid attention to it before, don't balance their checkbooks, are supported by someone else or live in a cardboard box under a freeway underpass, just ask them and they will tell you what is wrong. Too many opinions are driven and/or formulated by the hysterical media and their agendas. The Media's job is to sell papers, magazines and T.V. or radio time... facts, truth, relevancy and full disclosure not required!

So, what about you and those you associate with? What do you base your opinions on and what do you consider real wealth? Let's spend some time there and take apart some of the misconceptions and get right down to what it is you want and what it would take for you to consider yourself truly wealthy.

First, lets set some parameters:

1. True Wealth is personal
2. True wealth is not only about money
3. True wealth changes as you change
4. True wealth requires eternal vigilance, just like freedom does.

With this in mind lets delve into wealth and its components.

SPIRITUAL—Yes, this is the primary component. Until a person realizes that we are Spiritual beings having a physical experience, they will never experience true wealth. This is not a religious issue, it is acknowledging the fact that, as a created being, we are in a co-creative position at all times. Life does not just happen! You help it to happen, in a big way. We are created with a purpose and intent, not just by some cosmic accident. Being at peace with ones self and following your passion (what are your gifts and talents, what are you good at, what would you do for free just for the sheer joy of it???), all these questions must be dealt with for a person to have spiritual wealth.

PHYSICAL—Health: having a strong, flexible body with great stamina and vibrant energy. The ability to do what you choose to do without physical limitations is something to work toward. Superman is a cartoon character but living a life that is energy filled, clear headed with a body that is not constantly complaining or breaking down is not a fantasy. It is a true blessing and we are responsible for our part in making it happen.

There are a few common sense things we can do. Eat better, I don't mean just eat green algae and Brazilian roots. I am a 70-30 eater. Most of what I eat is good for me, but I realize that pizza is part of the basic food groups and should be consumed once in a while, just not three times a week! I take good supplements; I truly enjoy working out and running. Do I do it as a strict calendar issue? Not really, but I do it! I do what I can to avoid inappropriate stress. I make sure I have down time and relax. And, recently, I have added a most amazing feature to my diet.

I purchased a Kangen water system and it is fabulous! It is truly healthy, hydrating, high alkalinity, energizing water. After all, water is the most common component in our bodies. It makes sense to drink the best. Check out this website and decide for yourself. I did lots of research and feel strongly about my decision, www.thatwatergal.com.

FINANCIAL—Here is where most people think wealth lies. It does, in part. Lots of money is good, lots of money without peace, health, relationships, etc. Not good!

First key, know what you love to do, figure out a way to turn that into a business or paycheck and you will NEVER WORK AGAIN! Second key, learn about leverage, how to do something just once or twice and be paid on it repeatedly. Third key, stay creative, don't concern yourself with competition. There is enough abundance for everyone to prosper. Fourth key, learn about multiple streams of income. Every truly wealthy person has more that one source of revenue, you can too. Remember, before you jump into anything, do your homework and work with someone you can believe in and with those you can trust. I have very little in the bank, just enough. Banks are lousy places to keep lots of money! The rest is working for me as hard as I worked for it!

Invest wisely. If the masses are doing X, I recommend you do Y. The masses don't get wealthy. Individuals do. Find someone who is doing or prospering in a manner you would feel comfortable with and ask him or her what it is that he or she is doing. Wealthy people not only think differently but also do things differently than most people.

45

They didn't get financially wealthy doing too many dumb things.

SOCIAL/RELATIONAL—Surrounding yourself with wonderful, caring people is a source of true wealth. Find like-minded people to associate with—not those who necessary agree with you—but who at least have the same mind-set. Guard, protect and nurture these relationships. They are deserving of respect and are truly worth gold.

Spend time in developing your social/communication skills. You will attract the type of person that you are or are becoming. This time spent pays out the highest dividends. Investing in your self always does.

FUTURE PURPOSE—An exciting outlook on what the future holds is important. Being optimistic about what the future promises is critical for someone to wake up each day and look forward to the next 24 hours. As a co-creator in this process, much of the responsibility for tomorrow is on your plate. The universe is neither whimsical nor chaotic. There are laws and they respond to anybody that knows them. When you fully grasp this you will find a renewed enthusiasm for the rest of your life. This is true wealth. What is possible and available for you, your business and all else is a blank canvas. Paint it in the most vibrant life-filled colors you can come up with. You are the artist of your life!

EMOTIONAL—In today's crazy, speed freak, hyped up, super-sonic style of life, it comes as no surprise that just in the United States there are enough antidepressant prescriptions written to cover every American man, woman and child, annually. I have seen grown adults (for teenagers, this is normal) start to have mild fits and actually begin to sweat if you ask them to shut off their phones for longer than one hour. Overhearing phone conversations in toilet stalls is no longer unusual!

Peaceful, calm and meditative times even cause stress. They cause stress because people have to work so hard to make the time happen! Imagine, you get frantic just so that you can relax. Is it just me, or do you to see just a bit of irony here?

Let me encourage you to do what it takes to treat yourself to truly healthy mental experiences. Go for walks (without your phone), watch trees be green, play with little kids in the water, mud or park, grow a garden, get full body massages, shut off the T.V! You get the idea. Enjoy the wealth you are creating; otherwise, you can just die of high blood pressure and leave it all to someone else and they will enjoy it for you.

BE PRESENT—Yesterday is THE PAST, tomorrow is THE FUTURE, all you have is THE GIFT OF THE PRESENT. Experience the moment. It is now that life is happening. You can't drive forward looking in a rear view mirror and you can't spend time in what is to come. The present is the place for creation and experiencing! Time is your most valuable commodity and once spent, it is forever gone. So, don't waste it, invest it!

True wealth allows you to savor every moment, enjoy

each bite of a delicious meal, listen to your favorite music more than once, hug your loved ones for no reason, take the long way to your destination because of the view and NOT DO ANYTHING because you don't have to. This is not wasting time! Wealth should allow you to choose what you want to do with your time. When was the last time you sat in a beautiful location and had enough time to experience REAL THOUGHT! Ponder this, allowing yourself time for uninterrupted, free flowing, creative thought sounds almost magical, doesn't it? Only you can create that, and believe me, it is a vital component of true wealth.

I end with these few words of encouragement: Focus on the desired results, emphasize quality of time and lifestyle, guard your decisions, and then mentor others to do the same. Why? I answer that with one of my favorite quotes, "I am looking for wealthy people, who are living lives of abundance, bringing good into their communities, who want to walk the beaches of the world together."

Want to join me?

Brian Tracy submitted the following article. He is the most listened to audio author on personal and business success in the world today. He is the author/narrator of countless bestselling audio learning programs and the author of 16 books.

Contact Brian Tracy at:
Brian Tracy International
462 Stevens Ave., Suite 202
Solana Beach, CA 92075
Phone (858) 481-2977
www.BrianTracy.com

CHAPTER FIVE
Leading and Motivating
By Brian Tracy

It's been said that "Leadership is not what you do, but who you are." This, however, is only partially true. Leadership is very much who you are, but it cannot be divorced from what you do. Who you are represents the inner person, and what you do represents the outer person. Each is dependent on the other for maximum effectiveness.

The starting point of motivational leadership is to begin seeing yourself as a role model, seeing yourself as an example to others. See yourself as a person who sets the standards that others follow. A key characteristic of leaders is that they set high standards of accountability for themselves and for their behaviors. They assume that others are watching them and then setting their own standards by what they do. They, in fact, lead by example, just exactly as though someone were following them around, surreptitiously taking notes and photographs of their daily actions for others to see and act on.

Motivational leadership is based on the Law of Indirect Effort. According to this law, most things in human life are achieved more easily by indirect means than they are by direct means. You more easily become a leader to others by demonstrating that you have the qualities of leadership than you do by ordering others to follow your directions. Instead of trying to get people to emulate you, you concentrate on living a life that is so admirable that others want to be like you without your saying a word.

50

In business, there are several kinds of power. Two of these are ascribed power and position power.

Position power is the power that comes with a job title or position in any organization. If you become a manager in a company, you automatically have certain powers and privileges that go along with your rank. You can order people about and make certain decisions. You can be a leader whether or not anyone likes you.

Ascribed power is the power you gain because of the kind of person you are. In every organization, there are people who are inordinately influential and looked up to by others, even though their positions may not be high up on the organizational chart. These are the men and women who are genuine leaders because of the quality of the people they have become, because of their characters and their personalities.

Perhaps the most powerful of motivational leaders is the person who practices what is called "servant leadership." Confucius said, "He who would be master must be servant of all." The person who sees himself or herself as a servant, and who does everything possible to help others to perform at their best, is practicing the highest form of servant leadership.

Over the years, we have been led to believe that leaders are those who stride boldly about, exude power and confidence, give orders and make decisions for others to carry out. However, that is old school. The leader of today is the one who asks questions, listens carefully, plans diligently and then builds consensus among all those who are necessary for achieving the goals. The leader does not try to do it by himself or herself. The leader gets things done by helping others to do them.

This brings us to five of the qualities of motivational leaders. These are qualities that you already have to a certain degree and that you can develop further to stand out from the people around you in a very short period of time.

The first quality is *vision*. This is the one single quality that, more than anything, separates leaders from followers. Leaders have vision. Followers do not. Leaders have the ability to stand back and see the big picture. Followers are caught up in day-to-day activities. Leaders have developed the ability to fix their eyes on the horizon and see greater possibilities. Followers are those whose eyes are fixed on the ground in front of them and who are so busy that they seldom look at themselves and their activities in a larger context.

George Bernard Shaw summarized this quality of leaders in the words of one of his characters: "Most men look at what is and ask, 'Why?' I, instead, look at what could be and ask, 'Why not?'"

The best way for you to motivate others is to be motivated yourself.

The fastest way to get others excited about a project is to get excited yourself.

The way to get others committed to achieving a goal or a result is to be totally committed yourself.

The way to build loyalty to your organization, and to other people, is to be an example of loyalty in everything you say and do.

These all are applications of the Law of Indirect Effort. They very neatly tie in to the quality of vision.

One requirement of leadership is the ability to choose an area of excellence. Just as a good general chooses the terrain on which to do battle, an excellent leader chooses the area in which he and others are going to do an outstanding job. The commitment to excellence is one of the most powerful of all motivators. All leaders who change people and organizations are enthusiastic about achieving excellence in a particular area.

The most motivational vision you can have for yourself and others is to "Be the best!" Many people don't yet realize that excellent performance in serving other people is an absolute, basic essential for survival in the economy of the future. Many individuals and companies still adhere to the idea that as long as they are no worse than anyone else, they can remain in business. That is just plain silly! It is prehistoric thinking. We are now in the age of excellence. Customers assume that they will get excellent quality, and if they don't, they will go to your competitors so fast, people's heads will spin.

As a leader, your job is to be excellent at what you do, to be the best in your chosen field of endeavor. Your job is to have a vision of high standards in serving people. You not only exemplify excellence in your own behavior, but you also translate it to others so that they, too, become committed to this vision.

This is the key to servant leadership. It is the commitment to doing work of the highest quality in the service of other people, both inside and outside the organization. Leadership today requires an equal focus on the people who must do the job, on the one hand, and the people who are expected to benefit from the job, on the other.

The second quality, which is perhaps the single most respected quality of leaders, is *integrity*. Integrity is complete, unflinching honesty with regard to everything that you say and do. Integrity underlies all the other qualities. Your measure of integrity is determined by how honest you are in the critical areas of your life.

Integrity means this: When someone asks you at the end of the day, "Did you do your very best?" you can look him in the eye and say, "Yes!" Integrity means this: When someone asks you if you could have done it better, you can honestly say, "No, I did everything I possibly could."

Integrity means that you, as a leader, admit your shortcomings. It means that you work to develop your strengths and compensate for your weaknesses. Integrity means that you tell the truth, and that you live the truth in everything that you do and in all your relationships. Integrity means that you deal straightforwardly with people and situations and that you do not compromise what you believe to be true.

If the first two qualities of motivational leadership are

vision and integrity, the third quality is the one that backs them both up. It is *courage*. It is the chief distinguishing characteristic of the true leader. It is almost always visible in the leader's words and actions. It is absolutely indispensable to success, happiness and the ability to motivate other people to be the best they can be.

In a way, it is easy to develop a big vision for yourself and for the person you want to be. It is easy to commit yourself to living with complete integrity. But it requires incredible courage to follow through on your vision and on your commitments. You see, as soon as you set a high goal or standard for yourself, you will run into all kinds of difficulties and setbacks. You will be surrounded by temptations to compromise your values and your vision. You will feel an almost irresistible urge to "get along by going along." Your desire to earn the respect and cooperation of others can easily lead to the abandonment of your principles, and here is where courage comes in.

Courage combined with integrity is the foundation of character. The first form of courage is your ability to stick to your principles, to stand for what you believe in and to refuse to budge unless you feel right about the alternative. Courage is also the ability to step out in faith, to launch out into the unknown and then to face the inevitable doubt and uncertainty that accompany every new venture.

Most people are seduced by the lure of the comfort zone. This can be likened to going out of a warm house on a cold, windy morning. The average person, when he feels the storm swirling outside his comfort zone, rushes back inside where it's nice and warm. But not the true leader. The true leader has the courage to step away from the familiar and comfortable and to face the unknown with no guarantees of success. It is this ability to "boldly go where no man has gone before" that distinguishes you as a leader from the average person. This is the example that you must set if you are to rise above the average. It is this example that inspires and motivates other people to rise above their previous levels of accomplishment as well.

Alexander the Great, the king of Macedonia, was one of the most superb leaders of all time. He became king at the age of 19, when his father, Philip II, was assassinated. In the next 11 years, he conquered much of the known world, leading his armies against numerically superior forces.

Yet, when he was at the height of his power, the master of the known world, the greatest ruler in history to that date, he would still draw his sword at the beginning of a battle and lead his men forward into the conflict. He insisted on leading by example. Alexander felt that he could not ask his men to risk their lives unless he was willing to demonstrate by his actions that he had complete confidence in the outcome. The sight of Alexander charging forward so excited and motivated his soldiers that no force on earth could stand before them.

The fourth quality of motivational leadership is *realism*. Realism is a form of intellectual honesty. The realist insists upon seeing the world as it really is, not as he wishes it were. This objectivity, this refusal to engage in self-delusion, is a mark of the true leader.

Those who exhibit the quality of realism do not trust to luck, hope for miracles, pray for exceptions to basic business principles, expect rewards without working or hope that problems will go away by themselves. These all are examples of self-delusion, of living in a fantasyland.

The motivational leader insists on seeing things exactly as they are and encourages others to look at life the same way. As a motivational leader, you get the facts, whatever they are. You deal with people honestly and tell them exactly what you perceive to be the truth. This doesn't mean that you will always be right, but you will always be expressing the truth in the best way you know how.

The fifth quality of motivational leadership is *responsibility*. This is perhaps the hardest of all to develop. The acceptance of responsibility means that, as Harry Truman said, "The buck stops here."

The game of life is very competitive. Sometimes, great success and great failure are separated by a very small distance. In watching the play-offs in basketball, baseball and football, we see that the winner can be decided by a single point, and that single point can rest on a single action, or inaction, on the part of a single team member at a critical part of the game.

Life is very much like competitive sports. Very small things that you do, or don't do, can either give you the edge that leads to victory or take away your edge at the critical moment. This principle is especially true with regard to accepting responsibility for yourself and for everything that happens to you.

The opposite of accepting responsibility is making excuses, blaming others and becoming upset, angry and resentful toward people for what they have done to you or not done for you.

Any one of these three behaviors can trip you up and be enough to cost you the game:

If you run into an obstacle or setback and you make excuses rather than accept responsibility, it's a five-yard penalty. It can cost you a first down. It can cost you a touchdown. It can make the difference between success and failure.

If, when you face a problem or setback, and you both make excuses and blame someone else, you get a 10-yard penalty. In a tightly contested game, where the teams are just about even, a 10-yard penalty can cost you the game.

If, instead of accepting responsibility when things go wrong, you make excuses, blame someone else and simultaneously become angry and resentful and blow up, you get a 15-yard penalty. This may cost you the championship and your career, as well, if it continues.

Personal leadership and motivational leadership are very much the same. To lead others, you must first lead yourself. To be an example or a role model for others, you must first become an excellent person yourself.

You motivate yourself with a big vision, and as you move progressively toward its realization, you motivate and enthuse others to work with you to fulfill that vision.

You exhibit absolute honesty and integrity with everyone in everything you do. You are the kind of person others admire and respect and want to be like. You set a standard that others aspire to. You live in truth with yourself and others so that they feel confident giving you their support and their commitment.

You demonstrate courage in everything you do by facing doubts and uncertainties and moving forward regardless. You put up a good front even when you feel anxious about the outcome. You don't burden others with your fears and misgivings. You keep them to yourself. You constantly push yourself out of your comfort zone and in the direction of your goals. And no matter how bleak the situation might appear, you keep on keeping on with a smile.

You are intensely realistic. You refuse to engage in mental games or self-delusion. You encourage others to be realistic and objective about their situations as well. You encourage them to realize and appreciate that there is a price to pay for everything they want. They have weaknesses that they will have to overcome, and they have standards that they will have to meet, if they want to survive and thrive in a competitive market.

You accept complete responsibility for results. You refuse to make excuses or blame others or hold grudges against people who you feel may have wronged you. You say, "If it's to be, it's up to me." You repeat over and over the words, "I am responsible. I am responsible. I am responsible."

Finally, you take action. You know that all mental preparation and character building is merely a prelude to action. It's not what you say but what you do that counts. The mark of the true leader is that he or she leads the action. He or she is willing to go first. He or she sets the example and acts as the role model. He or she does what he or she expects others to do.

You become a motivational leader by motivating yourself. And you motivate yourself by striving toward excellence, by committing yourself to becoming everything you are capable of becoming. You motivate yourself by throwing your whole heart into doing your job in an excellent fashion. You motivate yourself and others by continually looking for ways to help others to improve their lives and achieve their goals. You become a motivational leader by becoming the kind of person others want to get behind and support in every way.

Your main job is to take complete control of your personal evolution and become a leader in every area of your life. You could ask for nothing more, and you should settle for nothing less.

This article was submitted by Brian Tracy, the most listened to audio author on personal and business success in the world today. He is the author/narrator of countless best-selling audio learning programs and the author of 16 books. All rights reserved worldwide. Copyright © 2006.

Zig Ziglar is a talented author and speaker and has traveled over five million miles across the world delivering powerful life improvement messages, cultivating the energy of change.

Since 1970, an extensive array of Ziglar audio, video, books, and training manuals have been utilized by small businesses, Fortune 500 companies, U.S. Government agencies, churches, school districts, prisons, and non-profit associations, In addition, Mr. Ziglar has written 24 celebrated books on personal growth, leadership, sales, faith, family, and success.

To learn more, call (800) 527-0306 or
visit his website at www.ziglartraining.com.

CHAPTER SIX
A Life-Changing Procedure
By Zig Ziglar

"You can have everything in life you want
if you will just help enough other people
get what they want." —Zig Ziglar

That is my friend, Zig Ziglar's motto. It's not just a saying for Zig; it is, indeed, a way of life. Truly an American success story, he has dedicated his career to helping audiences around the world realize personal and professional success. You are about to read Zig's oath which reveals that commitment and a positive attitude are winning traits in achieving goals. Make a personal pledge to repeat it everyday, so that you, too, can begin to release the successful entrepreneur within you. - Don Boyer

My Personal Commitment

I, _____, am serious about setting and reaching my goals in life, so on this _____ day of _____, 20__, I promise myself that I will take the first step toward setting those goals.

I am willing to exchange temporary pleasures in the pursuit of happiness and the striving for excellence in the pursuit of my goals. I am willing to discipline my physical and emotional appetites to reach the long-range goals of happiness and accomplishment. I recognize that to reach my goals I must grow personally and have the right mental attitude, so I promise to specifically increase my knowledge in my chosen field and regularly read positive growth books and magazines. I will also attend lectures and seminars, and take courses in personal growth and development. I will utilize my time more effectively by enrolling in Automobile University and listening to motivational and educational recordings while driving or performing routine tasks at home or in the yard. I will keep a list of my activities, including the completion dates for each project, in my Goals Program. I further promise to list good ideas (mine and those of others) and to note thoughts, power-phrases, and quotations which have meaning to me.

Date   Signature

A Life-Changing Procedure

The eyes are the windows of the soul. So, to the person you are capable of becoming, each evening just before you go to bed, stand in front of a mirror alone and in the first-person, present-tense, look yourself in the eye and repeat with passion and enthusiasm, paragraphs A, B, C, and D. Repeat this process every morning and every evening from this day forward. Within one week you will notice remarkable changes in your life. After 30 days, add the procedure at the bottom of this card.

A. "I, _____, am an honest, intelligent, organized, responsible, committed, teachable person who is sober, loyal, and clearly understands that, regardless of who signs my paycheck, I am self-employed.

I am an optimistic, punctual, enthusiastic, goal-setting, smart working, self-starter who is a disciplined, focused, dependable, persistent positive thinker with great self-control, and am an energetic and diligent team player and hard worker who appreciates the opportunity my company and the free enterprise system offers me. I am thrifty with my resources and apply common sense to my daily tasks.

I take honest pride in my competence, appearance and manners, and am motivated to be and do my best so that my healthy self-image will remain on solid ground. These are the qualities which enable me to manage myself and help give me employment security in a no job-security world."

B. "I, _____, am a compassionate, respectful encourager who is a considerate, generous, gentle, patient, caring, sensitive, personable, attentive, fun-loving person. I am a supportive, giving, and forgiving, clean, kind, unselfish, affectionate, loving, family-oriented, human being; and I am a sincere and open-minded good listener and a good-finder who is trustworthy; these are the qualities which enable me to build good relationships with my associates, neighbor, mate and family."

C. "I _____, am a person of integrity, with the faith and wisdom to know what I should do and the courage and convictions to follow through. I have the vision to manage myself and to lead others. I am authoritative, confident, and humbly grateful for the opportunity life offers me. I am fair, flexible, resourceful, creative, knowledgeable, decisive and an extra-miler with a servant's attitude who communicates well with others. I am a consistent, pragmatic teacher with character and a finely-tuned sense of humor. I am an honorable person and am balanced in my personal, family and business life and have a passion for being, doing, and learning more today so I can be, do, and have more tomorrow."

D. "These are the qualities of the winner I was born to be and I am fully committed to developing these marvelous qualities with which I have been entrusted. Tonight, I'm going to sleep wonderfully well. I will dream powerful, positive dreams; I will awaken energized and refreshed; tomorrow is going to be magnificent; and my future is unlimited.

Recognizing, claiming, and developing these qualities which I already have gives me a legitimate chance to be happier, healthier, more prosperous, more secure, have more friends, greater peace of mind, better family relationships, and legitimate hope that the future will be even better."

Repeat the process the next morning and close by saying, "These are the qualities of the winner I was born to be, and I will develop and use these qualities to achieve my worthy objectives. Today is a brand new day and it is mine to use in a marvelously productive way."

After 30 days, add the next step: Choose your strongest quality and the one you feel needs the most work. Example: Strongest—-honest. Needs most work—-organized.

On a separate 3 x 5 card, print: "I _____, am a completely honest person, and every day I am getting better at being organized."

Keep this 3 x 5 card handy and read it out loud, at every opportunity, for one week. Repeat this process with the second strongest quality and the second one which needs the most work. Do this until you've completed the entire list. Use this self-talk procedure as long as you want to get more of the things money will buy and all of the things money won't buy.

Note: Because of some painful experiences in the past (betrayal, abuse, etc.) there might be a word or two that brings back unpleasant memories (example: discipline). Eliminate the word or substitute another word.

 **Elizabeth E. George, M.A.,** has asked herself how could an award-winning businesswoman and world-class athlete, have been so unsuccessful in her first two attempts at marriage? Consider her accomplishments: "Top 40 Business Executive Under the Age of 40"...Master's degree in HRM...CEO of Prefix Solutions Inc....Economic Development/ Tourism consultant ...University professor ...World Champion in Crossbow ...U.S. International Shooting Team 5-time member ...Recipient of the U.S. Government's Distinguished International Shooter Badge, its highest award for marksmanship. Yet she badly missed the mark when it came to love. Why? Uncovering the answer was the turning point in her life, and the beginning of *The Compatibility Code* and her forever marriage to co-author Darren George.

Contact info:
Elizabeth E. George, M.A. – Relationship Expert
Professional Speaker | Co-Author of *The Compatibility Code*
Prefix Solutions Inc.
29 Dickens Lane
Lacombe, AB T4L 1S3
p 403.782.1415 | f 403.782.1417
egeorge@yourprefix.com   twitter.com/elizabethgeorge
www.yourprefix.com   linkedin.com/in/elizabethgeorge

CHAPTER SEVEN
The Compatibility Code: Take Control of Your Love Life—Take Control of Your Happiness
By Elizabeth E. George, M.A.

"Marital success is the most important single influence on life satisfaction." [1]

Have you ever suffered from loss of self-esteem, even depression, because you were experiencing difficulties in your love relationship? You're not alone. Most people don't realize that the quality of their marriage is the single most important factor in their happiness and satisfaction.

It's splendid to be in love, and I'm the first one to agree. Men and women alike have grown up on a steady diet of fairy tales that started with "once upon a time" and ended in "happily ever after." That same fairy-tale idea showed up again and again in novels, songs, movies… and we came to believe marriage was simply a continuation of the fairy tale, where everything would be wonderful because we were in love.

All too soon, reality comes crashing down on us making it impossible to ignore that maybe love by itself is not enough. The consequences of not making smart choices have resulted in a 50 percent divorce rate. Some research suggests that as few as 20 percent of marriages are actually happy. Unfortunately, this leaves a lot of couples living in silent agony. I can't stress this enough. Culturally, the "love" approach has led to pain, grief, financial loss, frustration, and deterioration of self-esteem. The end result is that we have a lot of dissatisfied and disillusioned people out there, and they may or may not be aware that a source of their unhappiness lies in their love life. The simple answer to this mess is to improve the quality of one's intimate relationship. But how do you do that?

We have, for far too long, used love as the leading criteria for marriage. Currently, we attach even greater importance to being in love as a prerequisite to marraige than people did in past decades.[2] At this rate, nothing will change and our failures in marriage will continue to rip us apart.

Fortunately, as it turns out, love—sweet intoxicating love—is not the problem. It's using love as a way to determine partner compatibility that's the problem. Our belief in the power of love has become so fierce that we often ignore huge and conflicting differences, relying instead, on our response to a kiss or how we feel when we're with our lover. But the hard fact of divorce—and this applies to everyone: male, female, married, divorced, single—is that incompatibilities will destroy the most passionate and intense of emotions.

And that's what we're going to talk about in this particular mastermind meeting. I want to introduce you to a process, a code that will hopefully shake up some of your ideas about relationship selection and challenge your perceptions and expectations of love. While you can find the full conversation in my book, *The Compatibility Code*, here I will encourage you that there is hope, that there is another, better way to go about love, using a process that has an element of control in it.

The goal is to help you turn your fixation with love into a "prefixation" with compatibility—so you can take control of the love process and boost your ability to be satisfied and happy in life. To achieve this goal I'll first take you off the hook of expectation that you have to be a prince charming with a kingdom or a princess that needs to be rescued. I will then help you recognize you're already equipped to make good relationship choices.

Finally, before we get into the heart of the matter, as people who are systematically engaged in self-development, we're used to being prompted to be open to trying new approaches. However, I am also well aware that in the area of relationships, even though we've attempted to improve our ability to make the right choices about love, we may have lost our confidence because we've been hurt too many times. So I must pose the question: are you willing to try a new approach, engage in a new thought process, so that you *can* get different results?

It's not serendipitous—reversing the ouch of the fall

Before you start along a new path to marriage, you need to recognize there are some improperly marked road signs along the way. At the top of the post is the idea that love is based on serendipity—the occurrence of events by chance. The sign you are least likely to recognize as misleading is the one that paints the image of the man or woman of

your dreams directly from the pages of a fairy tale—or
from the movie you watched last week (ouch). Finally, the
sign that is shaped like a heart with an arrow through it,
says that love conquers all—and this perhaps, my friend,
is the most dangerous.

There are a ton of references in our language that lead us
to believe that love is out of our control. We fall in love.
We're "head over heels" in love. We're addicted to love. The
heart of all this language is that *we have absolutely no control
how or when the path to marriage begins.* At the core of many
self-improvement principles and techniques is the idea of
learning how to be in control, in a good way, of yourself
and your surroundings. But if one of the most important
indicators of our happiness is a successful marriage, and
yet we have no control over how that marriage began,
where does that leave us?

Instead, we need to get off our horse or get out of our
tower and find new scripts that help us see what real love
looks like. In one sense, it's like we have a frame with no
picture. In other words, we have the legal institution of
marriage creating the frame but without a clear picture
of the components of a successful marriage, it's hard to
know what we're looking for, either in the spouse or in the
marriage.

Too many of us come from broken homes. And now after
years of a 50 percent divorce rate, we rarely encounter
a couple experiencing an excellent marriage. (If you
think "we" have a challenge, consider that our sons

and daughters images of marriage will be even more fractured.)

It has become critical for us to find positive images of real love. I recommend that you actively research and read about the foundations and components of a great marriage. Seek out good role models; look for marriages that are thriving, that contain reciprocal giving where husband and wife are assisting one another, mutually striving towards common goals, where there is an attitude of encouragement and support. That's the only way to put a permanent picture in that frame you long to fill.

On your new path to marriage, you'll find that the love you're really after is the result of compatibility. In our current world, we use the "in-love state" to tell us whether we should continue the relationship. This is the romance, that out-of-breath feeling we've been scripted by Hollywood and by our own dating to interpret as the height of love. This is where we encounter our culture's intense fascination with the idea of love-at-first-sight and instant romance. And it's addicting, no question. But we've got it backwards! Because love fluctuates and changes, it is not a reliable indicator of whether you can live successfully with someone for the rest of your life. Love not only doesn't conquer all, it is eroded and destroyed by incompatibility. And yet we use the "feeling" of being in love as our leading signpost to take the next step forward in a relationship. We need to change our approach.

"You can help yourself" or "Love Control 101"

Let's stop for a moment in our mastermind before we continue on our quest for achieving real and lasting love. I hope that you just had an *ah ha* moment. If you have, I encourage you to step back and consider all the ways this has influenced previous relationship choices you've made. When you come back, we're going to compare this to a business perspective.

You wouldn't really start a business based on serendipity, would you? When you are on the path of earnest self-improvement or business start up, you actively seek out mentors and success models, don't you?

Let's narrow this down further and have you imagine yourself as the boss needing to hire an employee. You wouldn't start by hanging out a sign that says, "Please work here." Rather, you would answer some questions before the interview process begins: What type of job would this new employee need to do? What type of experience do they need to have? What qualities would help them be compatible with existing employees?

Why aren't we asking these same types of questions in our search for our future spouse?

As my husband, Darren, and I grappled with how to explain this to you, we realized that we had been approaching it from two completely different angles: Darren, with a background in research psychology, me with a background in human resource management. What if we could apply good business practices to finding love? What if we aligned successful decision-making models with research psychology on relationships?

I know. This doesn't sound very romantic—but then again—neither does divorce.

So here's the million-dollar question: do you want to take control of your future success in marriage? Your future choice of a life partner? Your choice in love?

Better yet—what if I told you that you already have the tools to be able to do this?

It's all in what I call the prefix process found in the second stage of *The Compatibility Code*. Many of the elements will be familiar to you, and if you use them well and wisely, you can find out what it feels like to *become* in love as opposed to fall in love. And when you choose to become in love, you are better able to transition into real and lasting love as your relationship deepens.

Our first step in the prefix process is to help people understand themselves better by encouraging them first to "take a look inward." This is the same type of exercise you do within an organization prior to the staffing process where you analyze the company's strengths and weaknesses as well as conduct a job analysis to determine what needs to be accomplished. In relationships, this first step helps you find out who you are and what's important to you. This becomes a profile of your core essences that make you unique and special. It also helps you identify any fatal flaws you may have that could be devastating to any future relationship—for instance anger, jealousy or self-esteem issues. In other words, you want to examine yourself before you put yourself up on the shelf as market ready.

Once you've taken a good inventory of who you are and what you need to work on fixing, you then want to craft a picture of your ideal mate. In HR, we next identify what the potential candidate should be able to do and what qualifications they need to have in order to do it. This middle Pre*fix* step, "taking a look outward," is similar to visualization. As you create your image of compatibility it will help you recognize the right individual when you see them. Here you will also arm yourself with knowledge of things that can cloud your judgment—such as loneliness or sexual urgency. This pre-thought and planning process provides the vital starting point for successful relationship choices and ideally is accomplished prior to meeting someone.

And finally, as you begin a dating relationship, you want to be able to determine compatibility between you, much like the job interview. We call this step, "taking a look together" in your dating conversations. I like to think of it as a treasure hunt because you are seeking to discover and match each other's essence qualities, those one-of-a-kind defining contents of personal identity. On the flip side, you also want to figure out as many red flags as possible and whether or not you're going to be able to deal with them in the long term. Above all, you want to identify and confront, as early as possible, what we call "disqualifiers," the deal breakers, those things you know you can't live with. You wouldn't hire an employee who is "perfect except for" because you know that the "except for" is the very thing that is going to make that employee not work out in the long run. The same tough standards need to be applied to relationships because that "except for" is often the very thing that rips the marriage apart.

Darren and I have found that if we can encourage people to do these three steps, then they will be more likely to recognize the "right" individual when he or she comes along, and, more importantly, be able to apply good selection decisions before their emotions take control. Oh and by the way, if you are already married, going through this process can strengthen your marriage considerably.

Becoming in love creates forever endings

What you may not realize is that throughout our mastermind meeting, I have been helping you create a new language, a new script for love. Instead of falling in love, you'll plan how to become in love. It's a powerful concept when applied because it means that we have chosen this wonderful person we're with, using our own criteria, and we can then have greater confidence in the exciting emotion that develops between us. It also sets the stage to be able to work together toward common goals and shared purposes.

At one point, early in our relationship, Darren wrote, "I

want to not only write the book with you but to live the book with you. I want our marriage to demonstrate that love can last a lifetime growing ever richer." Our courtship, conversations, and dreams arose out of following the steps that I presented to you here. We applied the cold logic of finding out if we were compatible, sometimes only heartbeats ahead of experiencing the breathlessness of the "in-love state." I'm very glad that we did because the breathless moments do not fill the majority of our marriage moments. Instead, our experience with real love reveals days filled with our mutual commitment to each other and encouragement for each other in our shared purpose of helping others find sustainable love. We are compatible and we are happy. And in wonderful joyful moments—we are still in love. When love happens in this way, it is the most romantic, the most breath-taking thing to behold.

So is it all about love? In the end, it's all about providing a foundation and an environment in your relationship that allows love to flourish. Pre*fix* is the method—compatibility is the result. Then it can be about love.

---

1. Haring-Hidore, M., Stock, W.A., Okun, M.A., and Witter, R.A. (1985). Marital status and subjective well being: a research synthesis. *Journal of Marriage and the Family,* 47, 947-953.

2. Simpson, J. A., Campbell, B., Berscheid, E. (1986). The association between romantic love and marriage: Kephart (1967) twice revisited. *Personality and Social Psychology Bulletin,* 12, 363-372.

Mick Moore, "The Internet Entrepreneur", is an award-winning web designer, acclaimed Internet marketing consultant, author, film maker and key-note speaker.

Mr. Moore is the author of the *Home Business Success Kit*, the *Google Adsense Handbook*, *Internet Marketing Secrets Revealed* and *The Internet Entrepreneur*, and is featured in the movie *The Power of Mentorship*.

Website: www.QuickStartExpert.com
Website: www.HomeBusinessSuccessKit.com
Website: www.KillerGraffix.com
Phone: 619-226-2877

CHAPTER EIGHT
Two Heads Are Better Than One
By Mick Moore, The Internet Entrepreneur®

You've probably heard the old expressions, "The Whole is Greater than the Sum of its Parts," and "Two Heads are Better than One." These old adages still hold true today as more and more people in business and athletics are harnessing the power of several minds to solve problems, seek advice and achieve goals.

The phrase "mastermind group" was first coined by Napoleon Hill in his classic book, *Think and Grow Rich.* In researching his book, Hill spent 20 years studying hundreds of successful Americans, including Henry Ford, John D. Rockefeller and Thomas Edison.

Hill defined the "Master Mind" as "coordination of knowledge and effort, in a spirit of harmony, between two or more people, for the attainment of a definite purpose. Wikipedia.com defines a Mastermind group as "A small club of like-minded advanced talents who meet periodically for mutual brainstorming/accountability sessions as first defined by Napoleon Hill in *Think and Grow Rich.*"

To state it simply, a Mastermind group is a group of like minded individuals that meet on a regular basis to provide support, receive advice, offer feedback and share ideas.

Hill also said, "No two minds ever come together without thereby creating a third, invisible intangible force, which may be likened to a third mind." He believed that a group of like-minded, achievement-oriented people could dramatically leverage each other's success.

It's been proven that by combining the power of a Mastermind group, participants tend to produce greater results in less time than "going it alone."

Mastermind group members commit to showing up and contributing to the success of each other. They become trusted confidants who rely on each other for priceless insights, candid feedback, valuable ideas, encouragement, support, inspiration and motivation.

Mastermind groups are as varied as the people who make them up. From large corporations to small companies, Mastermind groups frequently consist of managers from different divisions or locations, internal client groups, or new leaders who want to further their development.

Some Mastermind groups are industry specific. They can be Financial Planners, Attorneys, Business Coaches, MLM team builders or Web Designers who commit to learning from each other. Small business owners often create Mastermind groups to develop strategies, share lessons learned and leverage each others resources.

Today, more and more people are harnessing the power of these Mastermind groups to help them think bigger and produce more effectively. This concept can be applied to business, social causes, politics, athletics, relationships, health, and the arts. By combining the abilities of multiple individuals to solve problems, brainstorm ideas, and develop strategies, it's been proven that Mastermind groups can create greater results in a shorter period than someone trying to solve problems on their own.

There are no rules to the size of your mastermind group. They can range from two to ten members. Any more than that and things tend to become more difficult to manage. Most groups meet in person if they are in close proximity to each other. But with today's technological advances and those of the Internet, many Mastermind participants that live in different states or countries, can easily meet via the Internet using video conferencing such as Skype. As long as the members of the group make a commitment to show up regularly and to contribute to each others' success, no matter how they connect, you have a winner.

As I've stated, the types of groups can be as varied as the people who make them up. However, creating an assemblage where members have mutual respect and compatibility with one another is vital to its success.

Members should have similar interests or should be in similar areas of business, like Web Designers or Business Coaches. Or, a group's members can have a common goal like making a movie, creating a book club or helping each other diet and exercise.

Stronger bonds are formed this way and the group creates win-win situations for all of its members.

When selecting members, only invite participants who

have a strong desire to succeed and demonstrate an ability to contribute. Your group will be successful when you have members who are passionate about each others goals and aspirations.

In the beginning, everyone in the group should understand there is a slight development curve in forming a successful mastermind group. As the members gets underway, they need to have open and honest conversations about the goals and expectations. These conversations build bonds and lay the foundation for trust.

Being a part of a successful Mastermind group can be an invaluable and enriching experience, both personally and professionally.

You can create your own successful Mastermind group by taking the following seven steps:

1. Contact select individuals you think make a good fit for your ideal Mastermind group. It's more advantageous if they work in non-competing fields and have similar interests. Choose people who will contribute to the synergy of the group.

An ideal size is four to six consistent participants.

2. Establish the group's leadership guidelines. There should be some consensus as to whether or not the group will have a facilitator or leader and what role that person will play. I think groups have a better survival rate if there is a facilitator in charge to move

the meeting along. Your group needs to decide if that role will be permanent for a defined length of time or will rotate among members from meeting to meeting.

3. Establish guidelines for how the group operates. Determine the date, time, length and location for the meetings. You may want someone to volunteer to host the meeting each month, rotate hosts, or meet in a restaurant or coffee shop. Your group will also want to establish some "rules of the road," like issues of confidentiality, respect, how or if you share info about colleagues or other businesses, etc. Keep the rules short, simple, and clear to maximize the effectiveness of your group.

4. Formulate a plan. Set a general agenda for the meetings. You may want to pick a topic or focus for each meeting, from discussing tax strategies to valuable resources you use to evaluating each other's marketing materials. A set format ensures the meetings will run more efficiently. For example, the first 30 minutes could be open for general discussion. Then, each member could receive an allotted amount of time (15-30 minutes, depending on the size of the group) to discuss his or her "issue of the month."

5. Include an occasional guest (optional). Some Mastermind groups include guests as part of their format. These guests could be invited to speak on a particular topic (e.g., an attorney who specializes in Corporate Planning), or could participate in the planned format.

6. Take action. One of the benefits of a Mastermind group is built-in accountability. Be sure to take action on the ideas that were generated at the meeting. Furthermore, develop a support structure that includes follow-up reporting at the next meeting. Be sure to report both your successes and your challenges. That's what the group is all about.

7. If at first it doesn't work, try something different! Your first go at establishing your Mastermind group may start off a little rough. If some aspect of the group isn't working, be flexible and try something different until you find the right combination of factors that works well for you and the others in your group.

I encourage you to take a long hard look at starting your own Mastermind group. The energy you will get during your meetings will be a mixture of high voltage ideas, connections and support—second to none. You will be amazed at the results you can achieve in leveraging the talents and associations among your participants. Once it gets going, the synergistic power of the group will propel you and your business and that of your fellow members to incredible new heights of success.

For more information on starting your own Mastermind group, open an account on MeetUp.com, FaceBook, Twitter or the Forums online. These social networking sites are loaded with people just like you looking to engage in like minded thought and solutions. The power of the Internet makes it easy to connect and start your own Mastermind group and gives you a forum in which to do so.

As they say... "You are the Five People You Surround Yourself With.... And Your Income is the Average of Those Five People."

So choose the people you associate with in your Mastermind group very carefully. Doing so will improve not only the likelihood of success for you, but for the rest of your Mastermind participants as well.

Don and Melinda Boyer are national speakers and the creators of the mega selling book series *The Power of Mentorship.*

With power, passion and purpose, their mission is to help people create the lifestyle of their dreams. They are also the brains behind the two hit movies, *The Power of Mentorship - The Movie* and *The Art of Busniness for the 21st Century.*

Their Mentorship programs include 'How to Create a Publishing Empire,' 'The Millionaire Speaker's Home Study Course' and 'The Millionaire Speaker's Boot Camp.' All are designed to help you build financial independence.

The Power of Mentorship Training Center, where they conduct live seminars and trainings, is located in the beautiful historic part of Whittier in Southern California.

To contact Don and Melinda Boyer for any of their live training and mentorship programs, please visit them at:
www.DonBoyerAuthor.com
www.The PowerOfMentorship.com

CHAPTER NINE
Thinking with Passion
By Don and Melinda Boyer

My mentor told me many years ago that the only difference between a rich man and a poor man is his method of thinking. It took me almost ten years to comprehend and understand this golden nugget, but when I did it made me wealthy. You see, at the time my mentor told me that statement I was as broke and upside down as one could get. My thoughts about what my mentor had told me were, "How in the world am I supposed to know how a millionaire thinks?"

Let me shave off ten years of deep contemplation for you and give you the answer to that question. *A rich person thinks on the things they want and a poor person always thinks on what they do not want*.

Example of a poor mans thinking:
"I hate my job," "there is never enough money," "I don't want to live in this small house," "I don't want to be in debt," and the list repeats over and over again. What does this kind of thinking produce? The very things they do not want. This has to happen because of the great law of attraction. The law of attraction brings into our life everything we constantly think about: good, bad or indifferent.

If you want to become rich, base your daily thinking on your dreams, not on your current reality.

Example of a rich mans thinking:
"I am so thankful and grateful for all the wealth I now have: for driving the car of my dreams, living a life of luxury and having all the best life has to offer." Please note that this is the thinking that went on in their minds *before* those things appeared in their life.

If you want to change the circumstances and conditions in your life, it starts by changing the thinking that goes on in your head. You must think about the things you want, not things you have. If you think about all the things you have (which is most likely all the things you don't want) you will keep creating more of it. Forget about what you have and start thinking daily about what you want. This is the key to success, the key to getting everything you want.

As hard as it may be to believe and grasp, the truth is that riches are not the result of hard work but the result of right thinking. Some of the hardest working people in the world are the poorest people in the world. Hard work and riches do not make an equation, yet that is the illusion that the masses labor under. If you want to become wealthy you must drop the belief system of thinking that working hard is going to make you rich.

There is a massive difference between working hard and working with passion. Poor people work hard, rich people work with passion. What is the difference between hard work and passion? That is an interesting thing because both have very similar characteristics: long hours, government taxation and a 40-70 year commitment.

But here is the difference. Hard work will keep you broke, destroy your health, and keep you laboring at something you hate. Passion, on the other hand, can make you rich, keep you rich and add vigor and health to your life, while you have the time of your life.

Most rich people put in longer hours than poor people yet they cannot tell the difference between work and play, they cannot tell if they are working or on vacation. In fact, for most wealthy people, their passion is their vacation and often leads them to exotic places.

You see, this ties into another thing my millionaire mentor told me…

There is an easy way and a hard way to do everything in life.

The hard way which, unfortunately is what the masses are doing, is to try and do everything yourself to reach your dreams and goals. Melinda and I are firm believers in personal development and we have been students of it for 30 years. Some of our friends are the biggest names in the industry, however, the skills you learn in personal growth are not designed to create (wealth, success, happiness) but to manage that which you create through the law of attraction, which, by the way, is doing it the easy way!

Most people work to make success happen with hard work. But most of the time that plan only produces mediocre results at best along with an abundance of frustration and disappointment. Not a good plan to be on but that is the exact plan of 97% of all people. Will that kind of plan make you rich? No, but if you are one of the rare ones to accumulate wealth under that plan, just about the time you could enjoy that wealth, all the years of hard work and toil will take their toll on your health and you will find yourself on your way to the morgue.

What is the easy way?

The easy way is learning how to use the law of attraction on purpose and to your advantage. Most people complicate this law to such a degree they cannot understand it. But, here it is, plain and simple. Everyday the law of attraction is working in your life. It is bringing everything in your life to you. All the conditions, circumstances, events and people you find in your life are brought there by this great law. You may think that life just brings you random acts or events and that you just react to them accordingly.

However, that is not how it works; it just seems that way. The law of attraction works by bringing to us everything we think, meditate and focus on. If those thoughts are on the things we do not want, the law brings those things. If we think and focus on the things we want, the law brings us those things, as well. It is like planting a seed in the ground. The ground does not care or determine what kind of seed we plant, its job is to produce the seed after its kind.

Your job is to figure out what you want, not how you are going to get it. And it is the job of the universe or law of attraction to bring it to you. It is that simple and that easy.

Do you sweat, fret and fear when you plant a seed that the ground might not do its job? Of course not, you plant the seed and move on; it is not your job to make the seed grow. God created laws to do the hard part and gave us the easy part!

But, of course, the average person cannot accept that this is how life works and chooses to work himself to the bone hoping that this trail will lead him to his dream. You have no control over people and what they say or do but what you do have complete control over are your thoughts. And your thoughts are what create everything in your life.

Here is a golden truth nugget that may cause your mental noodle to smoke…

It is not doing certain things but doing things a certain way that will make you rich.

It is not the kind of profession or line of work you do that brings riches. People prosper and fail in every type of business under the exact same conditions and in the exact same location. You can become rich in any field or line of work. It is not the kind of work you do, but how you do that kind of work.

I remember, years ago, this one salesman I knew who made more money than anyone else in the company. Yet he worked less than anyone in the company. He did not do any cold calling or prospecting and when everyone else was on the phone killing themselves trying to make appointments he would be in his office with his feet on his desk reading *Think and Grow Rich*. It was amazing…when asked how he gets customers to come to him he would smile and just say, "I have a secret, I do it the easy way. I just think about what I want and it shows up."

Until you understand how the law of attraction works and operates, doing things the easy way will seem crazy, completely unrealistic and a total fantasy. The other option is work yourself into the ground, complain about your circumstances and do it the hard way. And that is exactly what most people do.

As one man told me, "No, I am not happy with the conditions and results in my life but, hell if I will believe in all that law of attraction stuff." This poor soul will keep suffering and struggling, not because he has too but because he has a peanut for a brain!

So we ask you, do you want to do it the hard way or the easy way? The choice is yours. If you keep thinking like you have been you are going to produce more of what you have. And that is okay if it is bringing you all the things you want in life. But if you find your life is filled with all the things you do not want and very little of the things you do want, there is an easy way out. Just make a daily commitment to think, focus and concentrate on only the things you want and ignore the things you currently have.

You have to have the things you want in your head before you will ever have them in your hand.

 **James P. (Jim) Noll** started his business career at 12 years of age. He began by cutting lawns for family. He wanted to save the money he earned to buy a car when he turned 16.

During college, he worked at the phone company and after graduating, managed a restaurant for a while and then went back to the phone company (AT&T) for the next 28 Years. He started out as a wet behind the ears CC9 Communications Consultant and, over time, came to do the things he enjoyed most: Training Manager, Sales Manager and National Accounts Manager.

One day, the powers that be decided his next career should start right then—but no longer with AT&T!

Upon graduation from AT&T, Noll stayed in the telecommunications arena with a position as VP with a private telecommunications firm in Los Angeles. They closed their doors and once again, Jim went looking for a new career. He found it in the direct selling industry—finally, no more phones! Currently Jim helps "boomers" and "almost boomers" with changing their health by changing the Water they drink.

Visit Jim online at:
www.ThatWaterGuy.com
ThatWaterGuy@sbcglobal.net
or call 1-800-513-3431

CHAPTER TEN
Where Do You Find Your Master Mind?
Or, Why Should You Even Care?
By Jim Noll

The Master Mind concept has been around for quite some time. Napoleon Hill in his book, *Think & Grow Rich*, published first in 1937, divulged the Master Mind concept in a chapter called Step 9 Toward Riches: Power of the Master Mind—Andrew Carnegie's secret to success. Napoleon Hill stated; *"Discovery of this principle was responsible for the choice of my life's work."*

The Master Mind as defined by Hill: *"coordination of knowledge and effort, in a spirit of harmony, between two of more people for the attainment of a definite purpose."* He also says that the Master Mind concept has two principles: the economic feature and the psychic feature. The later is hard to comprehend but understandable from the following: *"No two minds ever come together without, thereby, creating a third invisible, intangible force which may be likened to a third mind."*

Where do you look for the Masters for your Master Mind group? How will you know IF they are THE Masters? The Masters come in all shapes and sizes—with AND without accomplishments. *There is always something of value to learn from everyone!*

I believe that this very book is a great place to start your search. In fact, if you had every book in the *Power of Mentorship* series of books you would be in touch, and then

94

in tune, with some of the greatest Masters in the world of personal success and development. Other books by authors of great achievement and stature—too many to mention here—are also a great source of Master Mind material for your betterment. Consider this: if you were to read just 10 pages of one of these great books every day, by the end of the year, you would have read at least 10 books.

It is a very good idea to make sure that your Master Mind group is not all of like thinking. You need to include those with diverse points of view, both personally and professionally, along with different personality and/or social styles. For example, we once had a President who surrounded himself with too many others just like himself. That led to actions that were inappropriate and counter-productive and cost him his office.

I was first introduced to the Master Mind concept about 12 years ago by a very good friend. Because it was my first experience with the Master Mind group and concept, I prejudged the entire concept by my narrow view of the participants. I down played the merit of the Master Mind group without ever giving it a chance to work its magic.

I have since learned, fortunately, that a Master Mind group can *show the way* to better production and a greater degree of success than is ever possible through the efforts of one individual. The Master Mind group can also help to avoid some of the pitfalls that will take you off course. If you are willing and have an open mind, the Master Mind group can help propel you down the road of success at a pace much faster than you could ever achieve by yourself.

There are numerous reasons to make changes in the way you are striving to achieve your goal(s) in life. One of the most underrated is your close circle of friends or business acquaintances. Your Master Mind group can bring balance and clarity to your choices. Your Master Mind group can view what you may be too blind to see.

Inevitably, the time will come when changes to your circle need to be made. But, you may be too close to see—blind to the negative effect—of one or more of your chosen circle members. If you are willing to hear/listen and have an open mind to suggestions, you may find that there are those you should avoid or exclude and that there are those, current or new, you should seek. After all, we are the sum total of our five closest personal or business associates.

What if—where would you be—if you could spend quality time with the person… (you have answered this question at least a hundred times) 'Who would you most like to spend time with, living or dead?' Can you even begin to *imagine!* a one-on-one Master Mind with (*fill in the blank*)? My choice is always the man I had the opportunity to shake hands with when he was running for governor of California—Ronald Wilson Reagan!

Changing directions, have you ever had a Master Mind session with your spouse or significant other? Wow, what a concept. If you have an open and receptive mind, you will be amazed by the results. This Master Mind begins and continues with communication, a conversation and exchange of ideas in a comfortable setting—around the breakfast or dinner table, perhaps. Remember, we don't come pre-programmed with all the best ideas or best answers.

Here's some additional food for thought: have a Master Mind with your parents. What? you ask! I remember when my parents were THE smartest, most intelligent people on this earth. Then, of course, my view of them changed. Mom and Dad went from the pinnacle of greatness to become almost vanquished ones. What could I possibly learn from them? They are so old and not very progressive and, so on. Fortunately for me, that feeling about them did change. As age and experience crept up on me and, I took the time to communicate with them, I realized that they had wisdom far beyond my narrow, closed mind view. Today, I am thankful to have the privilege of having a Master Mind with my mom every day.

I believe that everybody has 'one' very special something to give. If your method of operation (aka: MO) is to prejudge, then you will miss out on that special something that just could be your 'missing link'. Take time to consider that thought—look for the 'one' special something—by occasionally looking back on your past acquaintances and situations. There may just be a gem waiting to be uncovered or rediscovered.

Here is an example of what could happen if you have a closed mind, or pre-judge. I once taught a class—SOCIAL STYLE SALES STRATEGIES, S4—from Wilson Learning Corp. The four styles were: Driver, Expressive, Analytical, and Amiable. It featured recognition of the social style of the prospect, then becoming that social style just for the sales situation at hand.

Social style sales strategies in the 21st century are radically different—YouTube, Twitter, BoomJ.com, Facebook, MySpace—are now the places where sales or connections are made.

What if you didn't, or you were unwilling, to evolve? Would it hold you back from your ultimate goal(s), dream(s) or desire(s)? Can you get where you want to be at an accelerated pace if you have an open mind AND were part of a Master Mind group?

You decide.

Lianna Marie is the author of several books including her bestseller about her mom's experiences with Parkinson's disease, *Everything You Need To Know About Parkinson's*, which has been sold in 33 countries worldwide.

Lianna is dedicated to self improvement, fulfilling her purpose, and inspiring others to find their purpose in life. She finds true fulfillment in helping those affected by Parkinson's and Alzheimer's diseases to live happier, healthier, and longer lives.

You can contact Lianna at:
lianna@liannamarie.com
Visit her websites:
www.liannamarie.com
www.allaboutparkinsons.com
www.yourguidetoalzheimers.org

CHAPTER ELEVEN
Ikigai: The Power of Purpose
By Lianna Marie

Have you ever read something that literally changed your life? Something that really inspired you or resonated with you so much you were left with the feeling that you had just found the missing piece in your life?

I was only fourteen when I first read Henry David Thoreau's inspiring words, "I went to the woods because I wished to live deliberately … I wanted to live deep and suck out all the marrow of life…"

Wow. Pretty deep stuff for a teenager, I know. Yet I believe those few words were responsible for helping direct the course of my life, and ultimately led me to discover my life's purpose.

It's because of my love for reading that I discovered this exceptional poet and his life changing words. By reading about people who are living life to its fullest, and about how to get everything from life, I have slowly learned why I was put here on this earth.

Twenty years after starting my journey, I discovered a concept that confirmed the importance of having a purpose in your life.

Ikigai–The Japanese Secret

Do you want to live a long life? Maybe as long as 100 years?

Or even longer? Most people, when asked this question, will answer yes but then add, "As long as I'm healthy."

What if I told you there's a place where living a long, healthy and happy life is actually quite common? That's exactly the kind of life people in Japan, and especially on the island of Okinawa, enjoy. In fact, Japanese people consistently have the highest life expectancy and the highest percentage of centurions (a person over the age of 100) per capita than anywhere else in the world. They also have the lowest death rates from cancer, heart disease and stroke. Amazing!

So, what's their secret?

Well, certainly diet and exercise are always important factors in longevity, but researchers believe that what sets the Japanese apart is their positive outlook on life and their sense of purpose; their Ikigai.

Ikigai is a Japanese concept that basically means "that which makes one's life worth living." This includes having purpose and meaning in your life and a joy about being alive.

A recent seven year study of 43,000 Japanese adults revealed that a person's life is extended when they have Ikigai. In the study, people with Ikigai were more likely to be happily married, well-educated, employed, reported lower levels of stress and were healthier than those who didn't have Ikigai. In Okinawa, the people's positive outlook on life and their Ikigai is also thought to explain their reduced risk of dementia. Not only does having a purpose help you live longer, but it also helps you maintain your good health.

Do You Have Ikigai In Your Life?

Everyone has a purpose in life; even you. You may not have defined it yet, but deep down inside you know you have one. So often we read about successful business people, professional athletes, the Oprah Winfreys and Tiger Woods of the world… and do you know what they always have in common? They have all figured out what they want to do in life and are doing it.

Because they have purpose, these people keep on going and stay motivated when others get tired or just move onto something else. To be successful in life, in anything, you have to have purpose. You have to have Ikigai.

How to Find Your Purpose

Knowing your purpose is a wonderful thing and can truly change your life. Purpose gives you focus and meaning, and gets you motivated and excited about life…you *want* to get up every morning!

So how do you discover your real purpose in life? I don't mean your short or long term goals, I mean the real reason why you were put here on this earth. The reason why you exist.

Here are a few questions I asked myself that may also help you define your purpose.

What do you value? What moves you to tears? What are you passionate about? What do people say you are really great at? What is your greatest attribute? (If you don't know the answer to this last question, go ask a close friend or someone you trust.)

I found it helpful to write lists. Even if you don't feel you are much of a writer, we can all jot down a list. Start by making lists of things you have always wanted to be, do, or have. This may include a career list, an education list, a travel list, an adventure list, a family list, a contribution list, etc.

Now take a look at all of these lists and see if you find any patterns. What do you simply *love* to do? When are you happiest? When do you feel most like *you*?

Discovering your true life purpose may take some time, so be patient with this process. You may even find out that your life or career path turns out to be completely opposite to your life purpose. If this is the case for you, don't panic!

If by chance your life purpose and where you're at right now don't really match, simply use your life purpose as a starting point to plan a new, more fulfilling life, career, or both.

Think of your life as a big novel, just waiting to be written.

103

When I was younger I read a series of book called *Choose Your Own Adventure,* where you would read a story that had different possible endings you could choose from. I loved being able to read the same story over and over and pick a different ending every time! Your life can be that way too. You simply have to choose the life you want.

For those of you reading this and thinking, "Yes, this sounds fine, but I'm too old to start on a new life path," consider this… Having a purpose can extend your life. So, even when you're 80 years old, like the Okinawans, you could still have at least another twenty years to live. That's a very long time and you can be, do, and have so much in that time.

Please, don't give up on what your life can be. Believe me, you can have it all. Yes, you really can. In the last ten years, I have discovered…

You don't have to work 9-5… in fact, you can even work from home, own your own business…and make your *own* schedule!

You can love your work…and still have time for other things…

You can travel to all the countries you always wanted to…You can improve your level of health through exercise and diet…

You can make a difference in someone else's life…

You can become pretty darn good at something, even if you start later in life…

My Purpose

It's taken me many years to clearly define my purpose and I still consider it a work in progress. I have many more years to live and discover new things!

If you are stuck on defining your own purpose, here's my personal example to help you get started.

My purpose in life is:

To live with passion each and every moment of every day.

To live with hope and optimism and to share this with others.

To inspire others to do things they thought weren't possible, especially in the arena of athletics and adventure travel.

To help others, especially those stricken with disease, through my love and compassion.

To live long, live happy and live healthy.

What This All Means For You

Here's the thing. Reading about all this doesn't mean anything if you don't act on it. Don't wait. DO IT NOW! There's still time.

"The best time to plant a tree is twenty years ago. The second best time is today."

So make lists. Find your purpose, and start living a life you love. Discover your Ikigai!

Susan Stewart is a stand-up comic turned Human Resources professional turned inspirational speaker and author. After performing stand-up comedy across Canada for five years, Susan then found herself working in a Human Resources Branch within the Ontario Public Service; long story. Throughout her career in HR, Susan decided to get back on stage and help people create habits that match their desires for health, happiness and success.

Susan has combined the two worlds of comedy and HR (and they said it couldn't be done) to deliver lighthearted programs on wellness, work-life balance, the powers of humor, and positive team dynamics.

Susan's writing has also been published in the Canadian book, *Awakening The Workplace* – Volume 3.

Contact Susan Stewart at:
1233 Yonge Steet, #306
Toronto, Ontario M4T 1W4
susanstewart64@mac.com
www.susanstewart.ca

CHAPTER TWELVE
Reaching The Laugh Resort: Putting The Powers of Humour & Play to Work
By Susan Stewart

"To be enlightened means to lighten up." – Mike Myers

The term "enlightenment" is much simpler than the word suggests or in which context it's typically used. If the status quo is challenged and a new, better idea is considered and put into practice to improve a situation, that is enlightenment.

Equal human rights, airplanes, and decent vegetarian burgers are all results of enlightened individuals. Major shifts in the treatment of minority groups and great inventions aside, another example of enlightenment is to challenge the timeless tradition of taking life extremely seriously.

For many generations now, there has been a conditioned thinking that being serious is the only way to achieve our goals and moments of fun and laughter are just forms of guilty pleasure that distract us along our path to success. However, after decades of this collective hunch that fun is the other "F Word," it's time to step back and look at the chronic stress epidemic and ask ourselves, "Is this belief system and way of being working for us?" Here's an opportunity for enlightenment—maybe if we lighten up and choose to have more fun, we could reach more of our goals and actually experience more joy along the way!

Would the new idea of laughing and playing more result in the reality that we truly desire for ourselves? It sure is worth considering as the status quo has presented some *"serious"* issues.

The same conditioning exists in the world of doing business. There has been a collective and long-standing belief system that a culture of humour and play in business is a diversion from productivity. Since the days the Ford Motor Company deemed laughter a disciplinary offense in the 1930s, the negative attachment to laughter and playfulness has been carried on throughout the years. It may not be said—but it is often subtly demonstrated—that seriousness, tough-mindedness, keeping everybody on their toes, furrowed eyebrows and employees walking around with the fear of God in them, are the classic sign posts of good leadership and strong work ethic.

Keep in mind that it's a way of thinking, not a matter of fact, that humor and play hinders productivity and decreases the chances of a business or an organization being successful. Here comes the same opportunity for enlightenment. Are the old belief systems and unwritten laws that cause people to have their personalities separate from their work out of fear that they will be viewed as unprofessional, incompetent or immature, working for us or is there a new way that will serve us better?

The results of the old belief systems about how work *should be* have often led to stress, fear and good ol' burn-out which are states that can stifle great talent. The other end of the emotional spectrum features peace, contentment

and joy (which are often results of humor and play) and
have the potential to propel a business or person forward
in ways that are just now beginning to be understood and
experienced. Putting humor and play to work involves
embracing and utilizing the lighter side of life *to enjoy good
health, to perform at a high level, to enhance your relationships
with colleagues and create new opportunities in your career.*

A brief announcement before we go any further: The terms
humor and play are not to be taken literally.

As appealing as lunch-time open mics and inter-office
softball leagues sound, the concept of *putting humor and
play to work* involve an extremely large scope of practices
that have very little connection to delivering punchlines
or organized recreation. Humor and play are expressions
of lightheartedness that raise the spirits of those around
you, cultivate positive personal and professional
relationships and develop your career. This is a shift away
from living and working in a fear-based environment to
one based on a much higher energy; and that energy is
love. Not hot and heavy love—well, maybe, but that's not
what this is about—but a loving atmosphere that helps
people maintain perspective and enjoy their time on this
planet. Think of times when you laughed, had fun, felt a
strong belonging, or felt safe at work and those are classic
examples of putting humor and play to work.

Are you ready for a change that brings about "chronic
peace?" Do you crave a shift in energy that lightens things
up so you can enjoy the journey as much as reaching
your goals? If you answered "yes" to one or both of those

questions, your definition of success has evolved to include the FUN FACTOR (feeling good and having a good time, too) and you're ready to *reach for the laugh resort!*

Humor, Play & Your Health

Have you heard of the mind-body connection? Here it is in a nutshell—what we think (and therefore feel), affects the quality of our physical health. When we produce stressful thoughts, stress hormones such as cortisol and adrenaline are released into our body and weaken our immune system among other not-so-good things. On the flip side, if we are in a positive, lighthearted state of mind, our bodies release health enhancing endorphins and other mood-calming neurotransmitters that lift our spirits and preserve our health.

The mind-body connection is a powerful thing and we can choose to take advantage of it by resisting the status quo of creating environments that are chock-full of negative energy. Here's the deal—stress is the "major ager"—it's the big roadblock between you and living the good life. Having fun and keeping it light (the antithesis of stress) is a key strategy to feeling well and living a long life. In a case study featured in Dr. Oz's book, *YOU The Owner's Manual,* it is revealed that people who have a sense of humor and have fun throughout their life now live between 1.7 to 8 years longer than those who are clinging to the old ways of taking life, work and themselves very seriously.

Bringing the scope in smaller, the mere act of laughter is just as healthy for you as eating a head of broccoli or going for a power walk. When you've had a good ol' belly laugh, you reduce your blood pressure, you improve blood circulation, you cleanse your respiratory system, your internal organs get a good massage (which keeps them healthy) and you burn calories—yes, that's right, laughter is a cardio vascular work out! Heck, you don't even have to laugh to gain major benefits because when you smile, your body releases good feeling chemicals that are normally very expensive and highly illegal. These chemicals are way more powerful than morphine so if you are a woman who may find herself huffing and puffing away in a delivery room someday, try to remind yourself to think of something funny that day!

The big picture about having fun and our health is that stress is connected to 99.9% of illnesses so anytime you're on the opposite end of the spectrum and feeling peaceful, you are putting a major health strategy into action.

Get the mind-body connection working for you!

Humor, Play & Your Performance

Do you have goals? Most of peoples' goals are tied to the outcomes that they desire for their life and work. Outcome goals are an effective tool when it comes to motivating yourself, but you cannot control all the factors that determine whether or not they are met. With all great plans for the future, there are some elements outside of yourself that will affect your chances of experiencing the things you want. Right now, it's the spring of 2009 and many peoples' outcome goals tied to their business, career or personal finances are being affected due to the current economic climate. The U.S. bank market is completely out of our control, but is a major factor that is affecting our goals, nonetheless. It's like Tiger Woods' outcome goal of surpassing Jack Nicklaus' record of eighteen major championship titles—it's a great goal to have, however, he cannot control the weather, golf course conditions or the scores that the other PGA Tour players post along the way.

The only factor that you or Tiger can completely control along the path toward your goals is your *performance*. To desire an outcome is quite natural and somewhat necessary, but due to the many elements outside of our control, the most effective goals are PERFORMANCE GOALS. For Tiger, his performance goals for each round of golf include his club swing, his communication with his caddie, his ability to read the putting greens and his level of mental toughness. If Tiger focuses his energy and time on those things he'll *increase the odds* of leaving Mr. Nicklaus in the dust.

Now it's time to contemplate the performance goals that will increase your odds of reaching your outcome goals. There are many great performance goals like communication, organization, and commitment, but to be enlightened is to consider if there are any new performance goals that will help increase your odds of experiencing success even more.

Sharing laughter with others and being playful in the way you do your job and live your life is an effective performance goal for anyone who is interested in working while being in a state of relaxation, confidence and peacefulness. Sound good to you? To illustrate the impact that humor and play has on your performance, think of the last time you were trying to achieve your goals while experiencing some form of stress. How was your performance that day compared to another day when you were having fun and keeping it light?

In the book, *The New Toughness Training For Sports*, author James E. Loehr introduces the concept of the "Ideal Performance State" which describes the extraordinary performance powers of a relaxed athlete versus an athlete trying too hard and taking it all too seriously. The impact of placing oneself into the "IPS" can easily transcend all areas of life and help you increase your odds of making your dreams a reality. When you can maintain perspective through humor and create a lighthearted vibe to work and live in, you are freeing your mind of the stress, anger, and fear that can so easily hold you back.

An enlightened performance goal for outcomes in service can also involve humour and play. Try combining your delivery of information and technical services while creating a connection with a client/stakeholder through some form of lightheartedness. Are there opportunities to share a story or make a personal reference that would evoke laughter or inject warmth into your professional relationship?

A Whole New Mind, by Daniel Pink is a book that suggests that our society has gone beyond the Information Age (due to abundance, technology and globalization—in other words, we've never had so much and the world has never been smaller) and we have now reached a new era that Pink describes as the "Conceptual Age." The "Conceptual Age" is a result of the countless options that now exist for a customer. For a business to be performing at a high level, it will now involve doing all that it can to create connections and inspire clients through the "human touch."

According to Pink, people and businesses will now see greater success when the gifts of the right-brain (that's where our sense of humour and play reside) work in conjunction with the talents of our logical left-brain. People are craving more than the usual delivery of information and service (been there, done that) so now it's time to consider the power of humor and play in creating a stronger connection with those you serve.

If you are in a leadership position, fostering a culture of laughter and play is a major performance goal that will contribute to the outcome goal of raising employee engagement levels. In Daniel Goleman's book, *Emotional Intelligence*, Goleman shares research that illustrates that leaders who are lighthearted are more effective in influencing their staff. The enlightened leader makes the leap in thinking that humans perform at a higher level when they are at ease and experiencing joy, so that type of culture is fostered rather than the traditional fear-factor methodology.

The "you catch more bees with honey" adage has been around for a long time for a very good reason—in all areas of life, people tend to want to please someone who makes them feel good and raises them up—end of story. When more enlightened leaders catch on to this not-so-complicated employee engagement strategy, look out! Just in case there is a leader out there clinging to the old ways for dear life as they read this, please note that one employee engagement study posted on the Internet found that people who were satisfied with their jobs, able to meet the demands of their jobs and had a lower rate of absenteeism, also reported that they had fun at work.

How do you get this relaxed vibe going? Lead by example. More people have fun at work when their leaders brings their own spirit to work rather than leaving it at the door each morning and collecting it again on their way out. Clinging to the old ways or not, think on this and try whistling while you work—literally—and it will be really funny if you can't whistle worth a darn.

Challenge yourself to consider new performance goals that put you, your peers or staff, into the "Ideal Performance State." Like the economy or the weather forecast for Tiger's round on Sunday, there will always be factors that are outside of our control when it comes to outcomes, so all we can do is increase our odds for success by lightening up, having some fun and seeing the humor in it all.

Humor, Play & Positive Team Dynamics

All high performance teams share a common characteristic and that is their strong technical ability is matched with positive dynamics that exist amongst the team members.

Positive team dynamics are a precious commodity—not because they're complicated—but rather because very few teams are willing to create the time and space needed to create or nurture them.

One of the simplest methods to improve a team's dynamics is through humor and play. When team members have memories of laughing and having fun together, they feel safer in being honest, accountable, encouraging, and doing all that they can to ensure that everyone is on the same page in terms of putting the team's needs first. If you have colleagues that you are close with and have shared some form of humor and play, are you not more willing to say something to them that's on your mind or pump them up when they're falling down? This is not to suggest that team members need to become best friends (or "BFFs," if Paris Hilton is reading this) in order to create positive dynamics, but relating to each other as human beings and taking time to just be silly certainly makes it easier to be unified when it's time to work together.

Organized play is also a strategy for improving team dynamics. If you've ever arrived early to a live sports game, you've probably watched the team do their pre-game warm-up. They create space and time to prepare their bodies and minds before they all try to win a game together. One of the busiest and highest revenue generating retail stores in Toronto, Canada, starts each day by gathering all the team members together to play a simple game before the doors open to their customers. This is an example of how organized play can raise a team's energy, create a rapport and foster unity. Using the method of play to strengthen a team is a great example of enlightened thinking in business.

Let's face it, there's got to be a more inspiring and effective way to start a meeting rather than just sitting down and looking at each other. *Organized play used to enhance team dynamics is definitely a new concept, but so was a decent vegetarian burger not so long ago.

Could a team that you are a member of be performing at a higher level? If so, is it a matter of lacking technical ability or do some issues surrounding team dynamics exist? If it's an issue of needing to improve dynamics, make a conscious effort to find ways to get the team to experience laughter and play together. Get the team talking and doing things that are completely separate from the work they do together. Laughter and play is how we learned to relate to others as children and still remains to be one of the most solid foundations that we can put into place for fostering positive relationships and working well with others.

Humor, Play & Your Career Opportunities

Another study featured in Goleman's *Emotional Intelligence* tested the practicality of academic studies that have attempted to measure IQ. The study led Goleman to the finding that IQ accounts for four to ten per cent of career success. Goleman states that the IQ influences the profession one enters, but it is a person's social dexterity that truly opens doors once in their careers.

In another survey study posted on the Internet, it states

that 84% of managers/directors said that their employees with a sense of humour do better work. This is a statistic based on perception and when you really think about it many careers are forwarded largely on perception. If you have ever been in, or currently are in, a leadership position, have you ever chosen to hire or offer an opportunity to one person rather than an to another, equally qualified person based on their positive energy, warmth and sense of humour?

When people are in the "dating scene" and looking for their future life partner, one of the qualities that is most sought after is a sense of humor. When people are playing the field, listen to what they focus on—they almost always mention something about wanting a partner who is smart, attractive and *fun to be around*. If people want to spend the rest of their living days with someone who values humor and play, then one can only assume that those very same people would like to associate with those kinds of people in their professional lives.

Enlightened thinking for career success is considering that humor and playfulness don't have to be left for attracting potential love interests—it's also a new way of being that can also make you *professionally* irresistible!

Humor, Play and Your Success

Fostering a culture of humor and play is simply about being responsible for the energy you bring to every situation and person you encounter at work and in life. The old ways of being simply have not involved that higher level of awareness. Past generations have been drawn into the illusion that each day should be limited to grinding away and achieving what they set out to do even if it means creating a stifling, negative, fearful environment along the way. Humor and play offers a new way that increases our odds for reaching the outcomes we desire through improving our health, raising our performance, enhancing our relationships with others and providing new opportunities for us to shine.

Keep an open mind and an open heart to experiencing the enlightened definition of success that suggests that it can't be achieved at all costs. If you reach your goals, but are left lying on the floor gasping for air or didn't have a shred of fun along the way, can we really call that a *success*? More and more people are measuring success by using the aforementioned FUN FACTOR which envelops feeling good and having a good time into what success looks like. Redefining success will be a gift we leave our children. There is more than one environment that needs saving and if we put humor and play to work, we are leaving a legacy of positive energy behind. When we look like we're trudging through a muddy field as we go about our life and work, our children receive messages that work and life are supposed to be serious and cause stress. Let's kick that old way of being to the curb and leave future generations another environment better off than we found it.

Enlightened thinking about success is to work away at your goals and, at the same time, be conscious of being a spark of light that exudes energy based on love rather than fear. Many people want to discover their purpose

119

for being here on earth. Consider that our purpose can take on many forms, and in whatever form we choose, our purpose is all the same—to be a source of love rather than fear. Reaching the "laugh resort" and *putting the powers of humor and play to work* edges us closer to living our purpose.

Send Susan an email if you would like her to send you an electronic copy of her collection of games designed to foster a culture of humor and play into teams.

Don Staley the 'Brain Cell Coach,' is an author, professional speaker, and coach who helps people get in the best shape of their lives, AUTOMATICALLY and PERMANENTLY, by teaching them how to reprogram their brain cells to create new empowering habits.

Don delivers a high-energy message on how to replace bad habits and create good habits to increase results. His passion to learn has propelled him upon a process of unending self-education and he has devoted over two decades to studying the thoughts, actions and habits of the masters.

Mr. Staley is a featured author in the Power of Mentorship book *Finding Your Passion*, a member of AAAS—American Association for the Advancement of Science and the CNS—Cognitive Neuroscience Society.

Pre-order his upcoming book tentatively titled *500 Days In a Row.*

You can learn more by visiting
book@500daysinarow.com
www.500daysInaRow.com
www.DonStaley.com

CHAPTER THIRTEEN
The Power of the Mastermind Group
By Don Staley, the Brain Cell Coach

It was 6:30 AM. I was in college and didn't have an early class, yet I found myself, not only awake at a time when the sun was just barely peeking above the horizon, but on the road making my way through light traffic heading toward a breakfast meeting. But this was no ordinary meeting, and this was no ordinary morning. On any other day, I would have gladly stayed in the warmth of my bed and grabbed a couple more hours of sleep... after all, there was a reason I didn't sign up for 8:00 AM classes! Just like that sun coming up over the horizon, something inside me had started to stir and had awakened a burning desire within to not only succeed, but to succeed in the shortest time possible after graduation. So here I was, 6:30 in the morning, on the way to my first Mastermind Group Meeting.

I first read about the Mastermind principle in Napoleon Hill's classic book, *Think and Grow Rich*. Most members of the group I was meeting with had also read that book. They had decided, with graduation looming, it was in our best interest to prepare for various opportunities beyond campus. This particular group had started before I was introduced to them. I met two of the leading members at a Toastmasters meeting that I had promoted on campus.

One member was the president of a popular fraternity while the other was a leading contender for "Mr. Bulldog," our "guy" version of a talent contest. Both were sharp,

122

energetic, motivated, and personable and just seemed like they were going places. I liked them immediately. They must have liked me, too, because as we talked, they mentioned their Mastermind Group and, when I expressed interest, they invited me to join. The Group, as they described it, reminded me of the concepts discussed in *Think and Grow Rich*, so I made sure I was available for their next meeting.

The format of the meeting was pretty simple. First, each person would present an idea, then the group would critique it, giving feedback and offering suggestions. The second part involved a member sharing what they had read. Each member had committed to read at least one book each month. One person would report on their book each week allowing the others to get a condensed version of the most important points. In essence, we were able to extract the knowledge from at least four or five different sources each month while only spending the time to actually read one book.

I was beginning to realize the true power of the Mastermind Group. Not only was I able to leverage my time and expand my knowledge, the synergy of those meetings showed me the potential power of a group dynamic. We were all working toward a similar goal of excellence and success. I was excited and committed. This first meeting opened a door and I got a peek into how the most successful people are able to succeed.

Successful people rarely reach that point on their own. Zig Ziglar, the motivational speaker known for improving the lives of many, was one of my first mentors via his books, tapes and seminars in my early days of personal development. In one of his audio programs, he talks about why geese fly in a "V" formation. It has been proven that when geese fly together, they can fly up to 71% further than if a single one takes the journey on its own. This example from nature reveals a sharp contrast to the idea of "survival of the fittest." While the geese work together to succeed, they also use the energy and wind resistance of one another to go farther with less effort. Many of us believe that if we are to succeed we need to do it on our own. The Mastermind Group works more like the concept of the geese. By working together, drafting off one another, you can multiply each individual effort and enable yourself to be more powerful and more successful.

This powerful group concept works well when you have defined the goal that you are working toward. According to a study by The American Society for Training and Development there are steps you can take to improve your chance of success. In that study, people who simply made a conscious decision to achieve a goal, saw success 25% of the time. When they verbally shared the goal, their success increased to 65%. When they included a specific accountability appointment, their rate of success jumped to a whopping 95%!!!

Just think, you have a greater chance of success if you work with someone (either a coach or other mastermind members) and verbalize your goals. Make an appointment with real timelines and commitments to that person and you are almost guaranteed success. This triggers your

124

mind to reach that deadline. Because you know that someone is expecting something from you by a specific date, instead of just "someday," you've added urgency to the goal. With the clients that I coach, not only do they get great satisfaction when they are able to tell me "I did it!" but I also get satisfaction when I see my clients win. So by sharing, you create a win-win situation. Do you still wonder why Tiger Woods has a coach?

In a general sense, a mastermind group is usually more than two people but it doesn't have to be. A coach or mentor and mentee relationship can also be a mastermind group as long as it's a win-win relationship and is working toward a common objective. This win-win atmosphere is something that top athletes, such as Tiger Woods, are well aware of. Do you ever ask yourself why someone who is at the top of their game still works with a coach? You may wonder why they would continue using a coach when it is obvious that they know how to play the game. It comes down to setting goals, keeping focus and accountability. A coach wants you to win and will hold you accountable for the time and effort that you put into winning that tournament, or achieving success in another area of your life.

I was recently invited by an Internet radio show to discuss the subject of New Years' resolutions. One question that the host asked during the interview was what a person could do to ensure that their New Year's resolutions would be successful. Of the principles that I shared, accountability ranked among the top. You simply must bring others into your "V" flight pattern to achieve success. You can hire a coach or mentor, get a buddy to hold you accountable, or start or join a Mastermind Group. This is not a chore, it is your life and your success and it can absolutely be much more fun when you are not trying to go it alone. In my opinion, accountability is important and can add great value to your life. It certainly has for mine.

As a part of that accountability, the Mastermind Group fits nicely. Whether it is a small group of just two or three members or much larger, finding the right combination can be more important than the size.

Currently, I belong to a couple of Mastermind Groups. We meet on a weekly basis by phone for about an hour. One group focuses on business issues, while the other has a focus on personal development. These groups are different; however, they are compatible. It is okay to belong to more than one Mastermind Group, just don't get too crazy because then you may find yourself spending all your time in meetings, leaving little time to actually DO anything. Your focus would get depleted.

Another benefit of the Mastermind Group is the connections you make. In my groups, I have met colleagues from all across the United States and even from different parts of the world. These are people that I may not have met if I had simply kept my goals to myself, or kept my circle of friends within driving distance from my home. The world is open to my success, and I am able to establish contacts beyond borders. And if you are wondering about whether or not Mastermind Groups really work, the answer is yes. From that original mastermind group from college, the three of us who were committed to the group were able to secure our ideal jobs several months before we graduated, while many of our classmates still didn't have jobs several months after graduation. Every mastermind group I have ever belonged to since then, has propelled me to the next level. If you are not in a Mastermind Group right now, I highly recommend that you find one or start your own. You will be glad that you did as it gets you one step closer to your goal, builds momentum and increases your chance for ultimate success.

Douglas Vermeeren is considered by many to be North America's achievement expert. He has interviewed more than 400 of the world's top achievers and, much like Napoleon Hill, has discovered dramatic tools for success in our day and age. Doug is also the creator of the film *The Opus* which most people are calling the sequel to the law of attraction film, *The Secret*.

Contact Douglas Vermeeren at:
www.DouglasVermeeren.com

CHAPTER FOURTEEN
What is Your Problem?
By Douglas Vermeeren

What is your problem? No really. What is the problem that keeps you from attaining your most cherished goals and desires? What is it that is keeping you from finding your greatest success?

Most people claim to understand the importance of goal setting in order to attain a better life, but in fact, approximately 80 percent of people never set goals at all. They talk about it; they recognize the importance of it; but, they just don't do it.

If you are not involved in an activity that actually requires you to think about and set goals, chances are, you've probably never really taken the time.

But let's say that you do set goals. Chances are pretty good you are still experiencing challenges. In fact, studies have shown that the 20 percent of the population that does set goals, roughly 70 percent, fail to achieve those goals they have set for themselves. And when you take into consideration the fact that most people aren't necessarily setting really hard goals to accomplish, why is it that these people striving for easily attainable, small goals are failing? It's a wonder that anyone accomplishes anything remarkable at all in business and in life.

Setting a goal is clearly something that many people just don't understand. They don't understand what it can do for them. They don't understand how to get started. And often they don't even understand what it really means to set a goal.

When it comes to goals, there are three categories: "be" goals, "do" goals and "have goals." In other words, who do you want to be, what do you want to achieve and what do you want to have?

Within each category—I found through my studies of top achievers—there really are only four areas that your goals can fit into: goals of wealth, goals of health, goals of relationship, and goals of self-fulfillment/ spirituality or self realization. Any goal you set for yourself will fall into one of these areas.

And when we set a goal in one or more of those areas it helps us to understand where we do not feel balanced or fulfilled. True success involves achievement in all four areas, and ultimate success can be measured in finding balance in the four areas.

As an important observation, it might be noted that "Be" goals always proceed "Do" or "Have" goals. Once you "be" it, then you can "do" it, then you can "have" it.

We've all heard the saying that "Actions speak louder than words." While this is true, we must recognize that "being speaks louder than even actions." In order to live a successful life, you need both "being" and "doing" goals in each of the four areas.

Throughout my career as a personal development leader I have had the pleasure of studying and observing, very closely, more than 400 of the world's top achievers. Some of these people have won Academy awards, Olympic gold medals, made billions of dollars, created world recognized brand names and have been recognized as humanitarians who have changed the world for good. They understand not only how to create balance and success, but have contributed incredible legacies and lived lives of fullness and excitement. It was this formula that I tried to obtain. How did they do it? How could I take those lessons and create similar experiences for myself with the things I was passionate about?

As I studied their lives I found several common themes. While there will not be time to share all my success principles and findings in this brief article, I did learn 10 simple principles why most people fail. I want to briefly explore six of them.

Avoid these roadblocks and goal attainment will be yours.

Fear of success and/or failure: Fear is the opposite of faith. Faith leads people to action. Fear causes paralysis. When people have fear they focus more on the obstacle or challenge, rather than the possibility of a positive outcome. What is it that causes fear? Often it is a result of past experience, conditioning and an invitation to step into the unknown.

While some people are afraid they will fail, some are actually terrified that they may actually succeed. With this fear they often unintentionally sabotage their own efforts. With this lack of belief in themselves and in their potential they never find balance in their lives and progress is hindered and slowed down.

Often they feel if they fail, everyone will think negatively of them. And if they succeed, people will be envious and think negatively of them. So to them it becomes a lose/lose situation no matter how they look at it. But the reality is far different. All top achievers have experienced failure and success. There are no absolutes in failure or success. There are only degrees to which things can be improved upon.

All top achievers understand that the only failure is when a person does not try. The lessons that will qualify you to continue successfully will come by the process of failing and succeeding. The greatest power in success begins in the belief that you can find the answers even when times may be difficult. Top achievers are not perfectionists, they are improvisers. Top achievers are confident that answers will appear for all situations whether successful or not. And, ultimately, success can become sustainable and enduring. Belief and faith are the solutions to overcoming fear.

There is a Zen proverb that states 'leap and the net will appear." This is very true. Always keep in mind that the worst and best case scenarios are never the truth. All is a learning process that will benefit only those who proceed in faith. Believe in yourself and your abilities, and others will, too.

Lack of understanding about the goal-setting process: As I have researched achievement over the last decade and,

Chapter Fourteen — What is Your Problem?
By Douglas Vermeeren

in fact, over most of my life I have found no less than three hundred different methods for getting to your goals. Many of them had similar elements. Most of them didn't work. Most of them simply didn't understand the laws of success.

Many of these formulas involved the mistakenly belief that goal setting simply means putting a goal on paper, setting a date for completion, marking off checkpoints as they occur, and then starting all over again. Such a mentality hinders people from success, and is incredibly far from what real-life successful people do. A goal isn't a one-time thing that you eventually scratch off a list.

Setting a goal is really about changing yourself for the long-term. Effective goals aren't short-term, quick-fix things; they are fixed and immovable destinations that show the world who you want to become or what you want to achieve.

Consider if you were on board an airplane headed for Tokyo, Japan. How comfortable would you feel if the captain came onto the public address system and said, "Good afternoon, ladies and gentlemen, we have a goal to get to Tokyo today." Would you want to stay on the plane?

Or would you prefer that he announced that you had "Tokyo as your destination today and we are equipped and prepared to get you there." I think all would agree the latter statement reflects the possibility of success.

While there isn't time to go through the process in

133

detail here it is important to observe that effective goal achievement includes thinking in terms of destination. It includes relying on the experience of others, gaining the training to be effective yourself and a degree of preparation that can only come through experience.

Lack of commitment to the goal: As I speak to audiences around the world, commitment is the #1 thing I see people struggling with in getting to their goals. They often say things like, "One day I'd like to do that," or "Perhaps I could," or "Maybe one day." There is no power in phrases like these. They are wishes; not decisions.

Only decisions can change circumstances. Decisions are very different than wishes or dreams. They are a committed statement that includes a first action. Decision without action is a weak statement of what you wish for. A decision with action is a step towards the final destination. And when the first step is taken the momentum to get there is created. With each further step forward the momentum grows.

Lack of commitment also keeps people from giving their best efforts. If you want extraordinary results in your life you can't expect to give only mediocre efforts. Extraordinary requires extraordinary. There is no way around it.

Inactivity: Why is that after setting a goal, writing down dates, and setting checkpoints, some people stop? Why is it that they can't stay motivated and excited about getting to their goals? This brings us to an essential part of achievement. And that is to get clarity about why you are pursuing that goal.

While things like vision boards and written descriptions of what you want help they are, in and of themselves, incomplete. They have clearly described the "what" you want. But that is not enough.

In order to have the power to attain it, you must discover "why" you want it. True clarity begins when you can answer the questions of "why do you want it in your life?" "Why do you need it?" The more important and strong you can make the "whys" in regards to that goal, the more power you will have to attain that goal.

So, the next time you are constructing a vision board, take the time to add the whys to your pictures of what. Write the reasons for why right on the same page and make them powerful and clear. When you experience a moment of challenge or wonder what your original motives were you will find great strength in going back to consider your original reasons for why.

As a side note: this exercise may even save you a lot of time and effort when you discover that some of the things you thought you wanted—you never really wanted at all.

Failing to plan: With the popularity of recent films and books talking about the law of attraction, it has become very common for me to attend an event and hear people saying, "I just put it out to the universe and it will all come together." While I do believe in the law of attraction and have seen it work in my own life, I have never heard any of my friends featured in these popular films or books advocate such an idea as this. In fact, just the opposite. In my own film, *The Opus*, Jack Canfield, who was also featured in The Secret, stated that "too many people spend too much time focusing on the mediation part of the law of attraction and miss the action part of the law of attraction. I always say the last six letters of Attraction spell action."

Once you understand the destination it is your responsibility to begin looking for how you can bring it to pass. You must formulate some kind of action plan.

Now, I want it clearly understood that it is very likely that plan will change as you begin to discover new insights along the way. But it is essential that you have at least some kind of path on which to begin.

I have always enjoyed sharing the thought, "The journey of a thousand miles begins with a single footstep." The reason I enjoy sharing it is because I think it is not productive. How much better would it be to say, "The journey of a thousand miles begins with a step in the right direction." Perhaps then the journey wouldn't be a thousand miles, and you would get to your goal quicker.

Direction can only come through having a plan. Just putting something out to the universe is much like putting a boat in the ocean without a way to steer it.

Having too many goals: This is one thought that I hear regularly as I speak with people. They have so many amazing things they wish to accomplish that they don't know where to begin. Firstly, I think it is a wonderful thing to have so many desires to create and explore. This is wonderful. But, as humans, we can only do so much and such a split focus will cause us to do nothing.

There is a Chinese proverb that states, "The dog who chases two rabbits loses both."

It's like they're standing in front of three bulls eyes with one dart. Hitting just one target is difficult enough; hitting three targets simultaneously with one dart is impossible. Therefore, it becomes necessary to determine the most important goal you are focused on and move forward with complete focus.

In my own life I look for things that I am most passionate about. Passion is a fuel that will keep you focused and interested in the goal, especially when challenges come. As I get clarity about the particular goal, I begin to understand what I am most passionate about. There are lots of things I would really like to do, but as I get clarity, I realize that there are some things that I must do or I would feel incomplete as a person. These things call out to me so loudly that I know I must do them and if I don't I will have regrets. These are the things that I look for. These are the things that I find bring the most joy, excitement and happiness into my life.

Search for those things. When you have those few key things then look at the goals that intersect with those things. What other desires are complimentary to those "most-passionate goals?" I will often then consider, from among those secondary goals, which ones are the goals that will give me the highest ROE (Return On Effort).

When I talked about return on effort I am not referring only to financial gain; that's not the only reason for doing something. In fact, I ask which goals will give me the experiences that I really want in my life or, which will create the circumstances that I really want, and so forth.

Conclusion

Goal achievement doesn't have to be an elusive target. You really can be who you want, do the things you truly want and have things in your life that you want. By balancing your goals into the four categories I mentioned and avoiding the mistakes that hinder people's results, you can achieve any goal you set for yourself and reach new levels of personal and professional success.

 **Kimberly Adams** was a tax professional for over 25 years and is a testimony to the fact that it is never too late to reinvent yourself. Five years after starting her own business, Kim was able to leave traditional employment to pursue her passion of owning her own business, helping others, training and speaking. Kim has great communication skills and is a dynamic speaker. Although Kim's background is financial, it wasn't until she started her UnFranchise business with Market America that she understood the principles of achieving financial security: leverage and residual income. Kim will help you to define your passion and implement simple steps to achieving financial independence. In addition to having both her CPA and CFP®, Kim is also a Nutraceutical Consultant with nutraMetrix®, a member of both Toastmasters and the National Speakers Association, a graduate of George Ramirez' Present with Purpose training and an avid road cyclist.

Kim is happily married to Lee and is the proud mother of Elyse, her daughter, and Brian, her son.

Kim can be reached at kim@kimberlyadams.org or by calling 412-215-6115

CHAPTER FIFTEEN
You CAN Reinvent Yourself!
By Kimberly Adams

Are you frustrated and stressed out? Are you making a living instead of a life? Do you have fantasies of tossing your office files into one of those large garbage bins and drafting your resignation letter? Well, this was certainly me!

You see, I had been a frustrated bean counter for quite some time. I didn't mind going to work and I liked the people with whom I worked, I just always had this yearning to have a totally fulfilling life doing what I was passionate about, which was helping and mentoring others, health and fitness, success principles, public speaking AND having the time and money to hang out with my family and friends, travel, and bike more!

As a working mom, though, I had two overriding priorities, Elyse and Brian, my two wonderful children! I was fortunate that in the accounting and tax profession, I had the ability to work a reduced work schedule so I worked part-time for many years. My career was a lesser priority as I enjoyed raising my kids and I also appreciated the fact that I WAS living my dream of being married and having kids without having to work full-time. Now that I understand more about the Law of Attraction, I see that I really attracted exactly what I envisioned my life would be while raising my children: time to enjoy them growing up, a way to contribute and adult contact that the work force provided, time with my husband, Lee, and time for

140

me! I wanted life/work balance and that is exactly what I got!

As my children got older, I became increasingly frustrated with what I was doing. I knew I wasn't really doing what I wanted to do. I have also been a personal growth and development junkie for many years. I think I first read *Think and Grow Rich* by Napoleon Hill when I was 20. I also knew that to be truly happy or financially successful, you needed to be following your passion and your bliss. I needed to start following my passions.

At this same time, my husband was going through some major health issues and I was faced with the fact that I might be the primary source of income for our family. On one hand I was thinking, "I can't do taxes for another 20 years!" But on the other hand, I was also very grateful for my well paying position and the financial security that we had created to that point so that I didn't have to return to full time work.

I also had a confidence or intuition that something would change.

So, it was no surprise to me when I received a call from a neighbor who asked me if I knew anyone who was interested in starting a business part-time. I said, ME!!!! I met John when I was cycling and I would see him and his business partner, Tom, in our local coffee shop wearing their bike shorts, often! I had to find out what these two were up to but I was following my intuition that something was coming my way. I'm so glad that I followed my gut.

John and Tom were tremendous role models and mentors for me as I started my business and remain two of my strongest mentors and very good friends to this day.

I started my UnFranchise business with Market America in 2002 and thank God every day for it. Even as a CPA and financial planner, it wasn't until I started my business that I began to understand that to create true financial wealth, you needed to leverage your time, in addition to your money, and find a way to generate a residual income stream. I understood about leveraging your assets by investing but not how to leverage your time. I figured that if I hadn't been taught these principles, who had? I became an avid student of the training system provided by our company which followed a franchising model. It centered not only on the specific steps to build an UnFranchise business but also on all the success principles: including attitude, goal setting and affirmations, persistence, the law of attraction and the law of association. I was already a self-improvement junkie, remember, so now I was learning great concepts on how to create wealth and my dream life but also how to help others do the same. I was in hog heaven! I have become passionate about spreading the word for what it takes to create wealth, not just in financial terms but also with respect to health and relationships. True wealth is having the time and money to do what you want, when you want and with whom you want!

One quality that has always helped me throughout my life is a positive attitude and empathy for others. I learned this from my first role models and mentors in life: my mom and dad. My mother is the epitome of faith and was always the rock of our family. My father was the compassionate, spontaneous and fun loving one and I am so grateful to both of them for all they have given me.

I am also a "reverse paranoid," as they say. I expect things to work out for my benefit and that everything that occurs in my life is for my spiritual growth. So, any time a challenge came, I would think, "What am I supposed to learn here?" I learned this from one of my mentors, Wayne Dyer. Wayne and I have never met but he is a "first name" celeb in our house. "What are you reading Mom? More Wayne?" Yes, honey, more "Wayne!" Wayne also taught me that everything in life is a blessing even though we many not understand why at the time. This helped me get through some rough times and to always stay in an attitude of gratitude which is crucial for creating the life you want. Study the Law of Attraction to fully understand this.

Something else that I possessed that was necessary for building a business and has helped me achieve everything that I have, is discipline. I have been able to set goals and accomplish them step by step. I decided to pass the CPA exam early in my career before the career's time demands set in and used self study books to do that. I had the exam passed two months into my accounting career. I went to night school to get my Masters and did it in two years by doubling up on classes. Later, when the opportunity presented itself for me to study for the CFP certification through my firm, I jumped at the chance, studied, and passed that. I love biking and decided that I was going to train for the MS150. This is a fundraiser for the Multiple Sclerosis Society in which you cycle 150 miles over two days. "OK, let's do it," I thought. I trained for that and have done it several times. I always have to pray for divine intervention up Cochranton Hill. This is in hilly Western Pennsylvania, by the way. I developed a passion for public speaking which led me first to Toastmasters then, more recently, to NSA (National Speakers Association) and above all to George Ramirez' Present with Purpose Course. This interest in speaking always makes me laugh because I took a zero in Mr. Ogline's 6th grade class on my oral presentation because I wasn't getting up in front of the room! And I was a first born pleaser with great grades so I've come a long way, Baby!

I was recently listening to a CD recording of Jeff Olson's, *The Slight Edge*. This really hit home for me. The *Slight Edge* is doing the little things to be successful that are "easy to do" but "easy NOT to do." It's understanding that every little choice you make throughout your day really matters, from exercising regularly, to eating healthy, to taking one little step toward your goal or dream. If I could help people understand one thing, it would be the compounding effect that occurs with your activities and not just your money. We all understand how interest compounds but we don't seem to apply it to our actions and understand that we also invest our time with activities that compound. One day of exercising might not matter but after 30 years of it, are you fit? Yep. When I look back on my life, it has been about slight edge activities—exercising regularly, investing regularly, reading regularly, and now building my business regularly—one day at a time. Take action every day toward your goals. Your actions compound and lead you to success in whatever you desire.

Tips to Reinvent Yourself:

Build belief in yourself. Building a business or changing course in your life takes courage and belief that you can accomplish your goals. If you don't have this, work on YOU first. Write and read positive affirmations to help program your mind and build your confidence. I heard a great comment once that has always stuck with me—"What your mind hears will eventually override what you think." This is great support for reading your affirmations out loud to yourself or put them in the voice recorder of your phone as I've done and you can listen to them whenever you get a free minute. And as my favorite bumper sticker proclaims, "Don't believe everything you think!"

Become a People Magnet. Read Dale Carnegie's, *How to Win Friends and Influence People* and implement every aspect of that book! It is a classic and time tested. Be genuinely interested in others and develop great listening skills. You will attract the type of person that you are. This is one of the principles of the Law of Attraction. Since so many businesses or any endeavor are about building relationships, this is a high priority.

Define Your Passions. What you would do even if you weren't paid. Try Janet Attwood's, *The Passion Test*.

145

Set Goals and Read Them Many Times Each Day. Remember, there are two types of people, those who set goals and those who work for them! Brian Tracy, another mentor whom I have not yet met, has great books on goal setting. See his *Goals* or *Eat That Frog*.

Enjoy the Process and the Journey. Brian Tracy also taught me that we are happier when we are working toward our goals rather than after we achieve them. You will always need to be setting higher goals for yourself.

Are you ready to reinvent yourself? All it takes is the desire and the commitment to make it happen—no matter what! Once you have this, there is no stopping you. If I can do it after more than 20 years in the rat race, you can too! Let me know if I can help you in any way. I am committed to helping you. Are YOU committed to helping you?